A GLANCE AT HERALDRY

THE ROYAL ARMS

Fr.

A Glance at Heraldry

by

IRENE GASS

illustrated by

CONRAD BAILEY L.S.I.A.

GEORGE G. HARRAP & CO. LTD
LONDON TORONTO WELLINGTON SYDNEY

To
The Rev. D. Ingram Hill, M.A.

First published in Great Britain 1959
by GEORGE G. HARRAP & CO. LTD
182 High Holborn, London, W.C.1

Composed in Bembo type and printed by
Western Printing Services Ltd, Bristol
Made in Great Britain

Contents

Acknowledgments

The author wishes to thank Barclays Bank, Ltd, the British Broadcasting Corporation, and the Institution of Electrical Engineers for permission to reproduce their coats-of-arms; the Chancellor of the Duchy of Lancaster's Office for permission to reproduce the Seal of the County Palatine of Lancaster; and the Vice-Chancellor of the University of Oxford for permission to reproduce the Arms of the University.

Colour Plates

I

The Origins of Heraldry

HERALDRY is the science which deals with the proper descriptions of armorial bearings (arms). It dates from the Middle Ages.

In that era knights on the battlefield wore suits of steel, with closed helmets, for protection. But when they were caged in this way, shut up more tightly than a snail in its shell, they all looked exactly alike. How, then, without help of some kind, was one to distinguish friend from foe?

So it became the fashion for each knight to display his own personal device, painted in bright colours, on his shield; and later, on the embroidered coat which he wore over his armour (his coat-of-arms), on his banner, and on his 'trapper' (horse-covering).

And that is how heraldry began.

It is true that shields had been decorated before this, but more as a means of adornment than anything else: the decorations had not been intended as signs of identification.

These personal devices were called 'charges,' and the shield was said to be 'charged' with them, and to 'bear' the arms.

The devices were very simple at first: a few straight lines arranged in a particular way, a coloured cross, a sheaf of corn, a sprig of a plant.

But after a time these devices became more elaborate, probably because the simple ones were becoming used up: the later the customers, the less choice available, it being a case of "First come, first served."

But it may also have been partly because the medieval knights, once bitten with the idea of a personal device, were no longer content with simplicity, and yearned for something elaborate.

Animals and birds came into the picture presently—not only real ones, but a whole zooful of those mythical creatures without which heraldry would lose much of its charm: the centaur, the cockatrice, the wyvern, and the dragon.

Some knights preferred to use a device connected with their own names. So the Trumpingtons displayed a trumpet, the Handcocks, a cock, and the Fauconers, a falcon. These are simple examples of what are known as 'canting,' or 'punning,' charges, and as time went on *they* became more elaborate too.

ARMS OF BOWES

ARMS OF LYON

ARMS OF H.M. QUEEN ELIZABETH THE QUEEN MOTHER

Perhaps the finest of all canting coats is that of Queen Elizabeth the Queen Mother (whose name before her marriage was Bowes-Lyon), which shows archers' bows and lions.

When all the knights knew each other's devices the risk of killing the wrong person or of being killed one's self was greatly lessened. So the fashion was not only decorative, but it embodied a sound scheme for safety first.

There are plenty of people ready to tell us that heraldry started long before the days of chivalry. They talk of the figures of ancient Babylon, of Japanese emblems, the Roman Eagle and the Danish Raven, the Norman knights as seen in the Bayeux Tapestry; they even take us back to the time of Moses, quoting: "Every man of the children of Israel shall pitch by his own standard, with the ensign of their father's house . . ."[1]—certainly a reliable scheme of identification.

The Roman Eagle and the Danish Raven, however, were national symbols, more like the regimental badges of our own time; and the device on the shield which the knight carried at the battle of Hastings was obviously a thing that he could change for something else when he tired of it; for in the Bayeux Tapestry, though there are designs of a sort on the shields, they are not heraldic, being the kind of thing that appeared in much earlier warfare.

ARMS OVER A CASTLE DOOR

What we may call real heraldry had to do with the armorial bearings which passed from father to son —a matter of family pride, and an indication of rank as well, since it was the knights who carried the painted shields, and not their followers.

A knight who had taken part in the Holy Wars would be proud of the emblem under which he had fought, and a son worth his salt would make it his

[1] Numbers ii, 2.

life's ambition to be worthy of his father's arms, which would in due course descend to him.

By the end of the twelfth century heraldry had become firmly established both in England and in Europe as a hereditary science; and in England, by the middle of the thirteenth century at latest, it had a set of rules and a technical language all its own.

Though shields were charged in the first place as a means of identification in battle or tournament, when this need grew less urgent 'coats-of-arms' came into use in everyday life as well. In the castle the coat was greatly in evidence, marking personal possessions; arms over a castle door would constitute a kind of medieval name-plate; at the village church my lord could see his arms on the tombs of his ancestors, on the bench ends, and carved in the stonework; they were there, too, in the stained-glass windows.

All this was very convenient in an age when hardly anybody apart from members of religious bodies could read.

As armorial bearings at first were placed upon the shield, the heraldic artists, when designing new coats-of-arms in time of peace, still pictured them as resting on the shield.

If the heraldic shield was being designed for a woman it took the shape of a 'lozenge,' which is a diamond standing on one of its angles, like the diamond in a pack of cards. The shield proper was connected with warfare, and naturally it had nothing to do with women.

Arms displayed on a lozenge

2

The Shield: General

THE terms 'armory' and 'heraldry' are often used as if they were interchangeable. Strictly speaking, armory applies to arms alone, while heraldry includes all those matters dealt with by the College of Arms.

'Armigerous' persons possess an 'achievement,' which comprises the 'shield' and its accessories (helmet, wreath (torse), crest, mantling, motto, all of which will be dealt with later).

The shield, often called in heraldry the 'escutcheon,' is the most important part of the achievement, as it bears the actual arms.

As far back as the Old Testament the shield was looked upon as the warrior's most precious possession. In David's lamentation over Saul he speaks of "the shield of the mighty . . . vilely cast away, the shield of Saul, as though he had not been anointed with oil"[1]; and the mothers of Sparta used to warn their sons to return from battle "either with their shield or upon it." To return upon it would mean that death had taken them in the fight, for shields were often large enough to bear the body of a man; but to come home *minus* his shield would have been a deep disgrace for a warrior.

The shape of the shield changed as the centuries passed. The Norman shield was shaped like a kite, as shown in the Bayeux Tapestry, and reached from shoulder to ankle, thus affording great protection; but it was not so suitable for displaying arms on account of its narrowness, except in cases where only a single charge occurred.

Towards the end of the twelfth century the kite-shaped shield gave place to something shorter and curved to fit the body; this

[1] II Samuel i, 21.

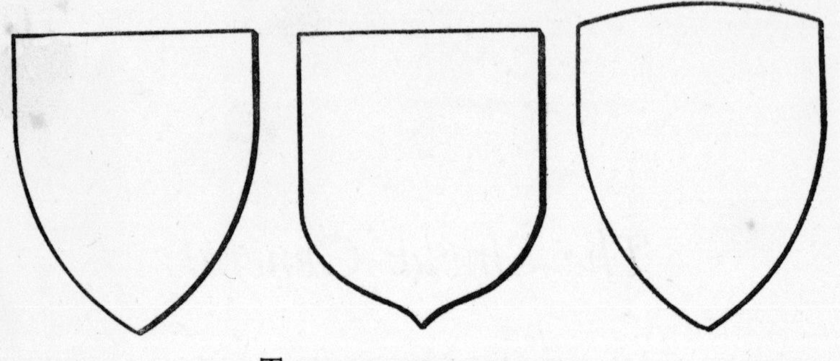

THREE TYPES OF SHIELDS

was known as the 'heater-shaped' shield. It afforded more space for heraldic display.

Most interesting of all, perhaps, was the shield with the notch in the 'dexter' (right) side, through which the lance was passed when the shield was displayed on the breast. This shield à bouche, as it was called, is to be seen on an issue of the half-crown piece in the reign of George V.

SHIELD À BOUCHE

The Points of a Shield

For convenience in describing the position of charges, names have been given to the various parts of a shield, and to specific 'points' on its surface.

The whole area enclosed by the edge of the shield is known as the 'field.' The right-hand side is the dexter, and the left the 'sinister' (meaning right and left of the holder of the shield, not of the onlooker).

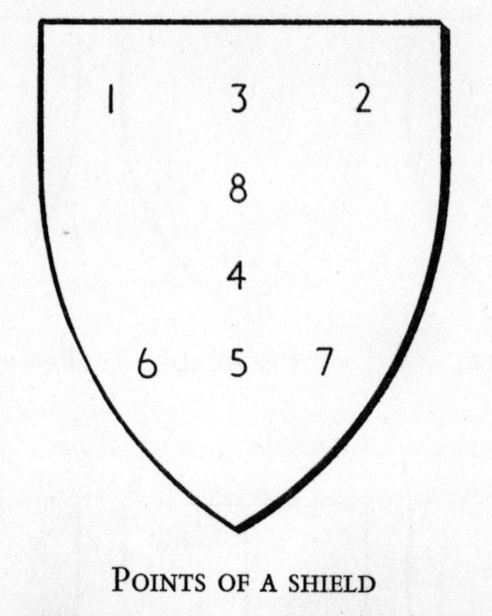

POINTS OF A SHIELD

1. Dexter chief point
2. Sinister chief
3. Middle chief
4. Fesse point
5. Middle base
6. Dexter base
7. Sinister base
8. Honour point

The top of the shield is the 'chief,' and the bottom the 'base.' The chief is looked upon as the most 'honourable' of the four, while the order of precedence of the other three is dexter, sinister, base.

The centre of the shield is the 'fesse point.' There are three chief points, as there are three base points. The 'honour' point lies between the middle chief point and the fesse point.

The divisions of the field are given below:

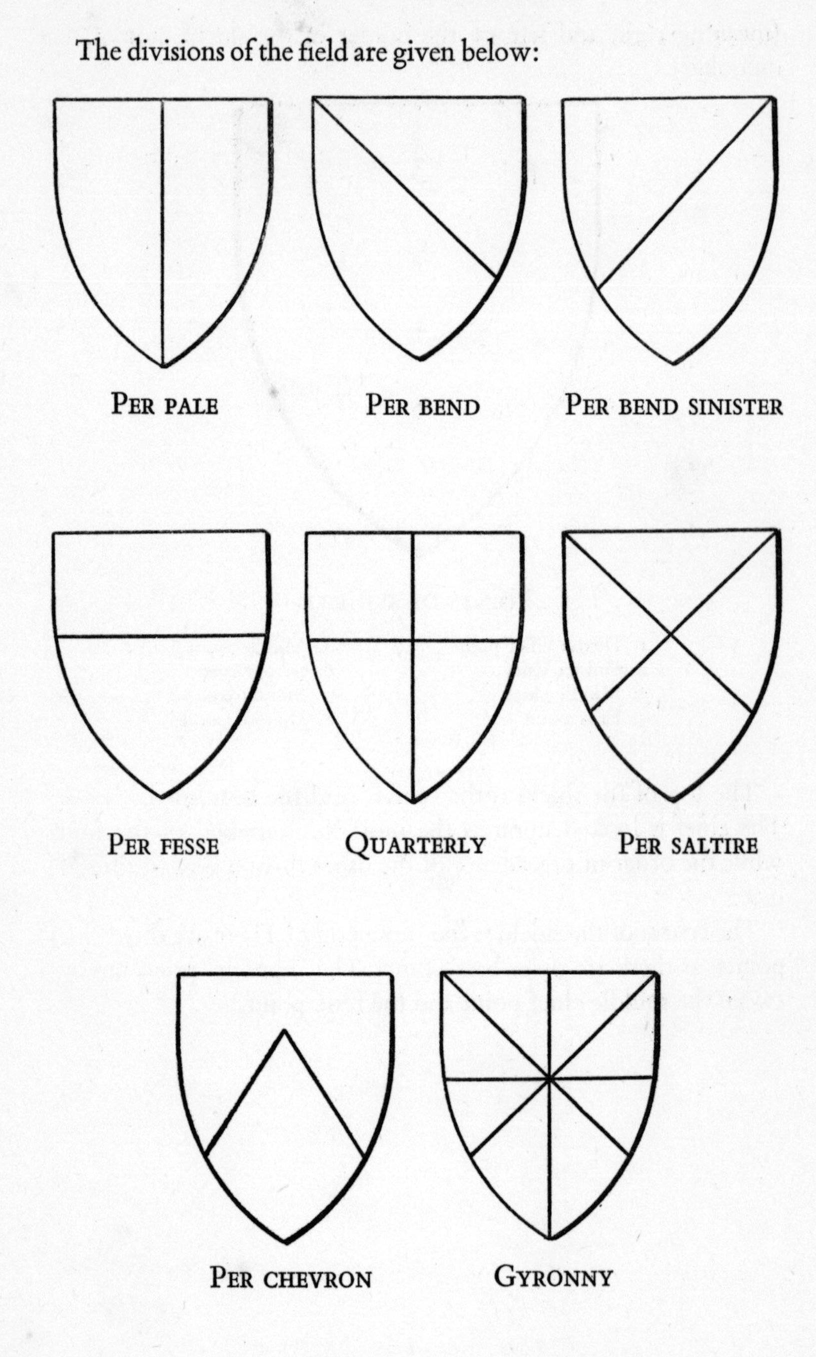

3

The Shield: Charges

The Honourable Ordinaries and the Subordinaries

THE most important charges on the shield are the 'honourable ordinaries' (usually abbreviated to 'ordinaries'). The origin of these geometrical figures, in use from the very earliest days of heraldry, has never been quite determined. They are three-dimensional, and are thought to be traceable to the pieces which were fixed across the shield from time to time by way of reinforcement. No doubt the "herald paynters" saw that here was an opportunity for decoration, as such pieces could be painted a different colour from the rest of the shield.

The main difference between the ordinaries and the subordinaries is that the former consist of broad bands which stretch across the field, whereas the latter are usually smaller, and often more intricate, figures.

Honourable ordinaries:

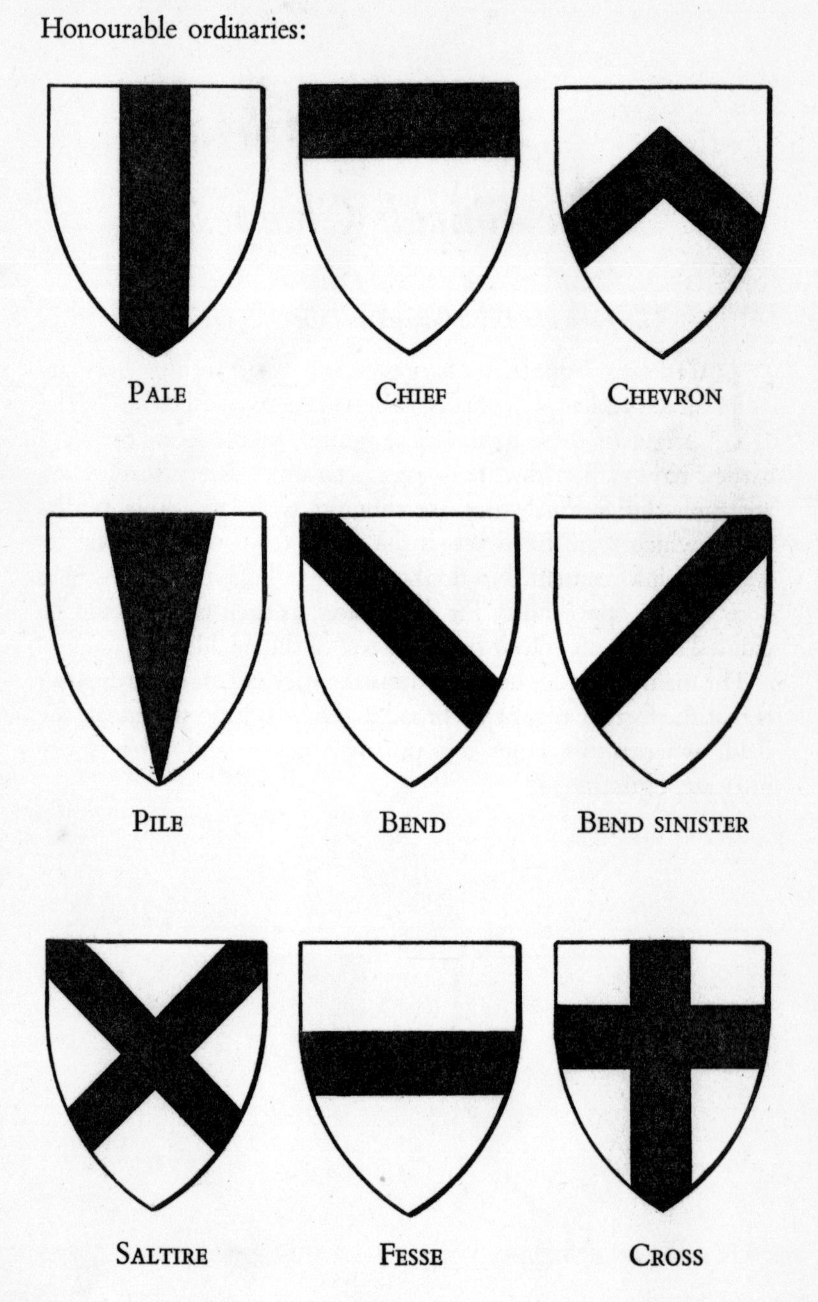

Ornamental lines can be used to vary the ordinaries. These are:

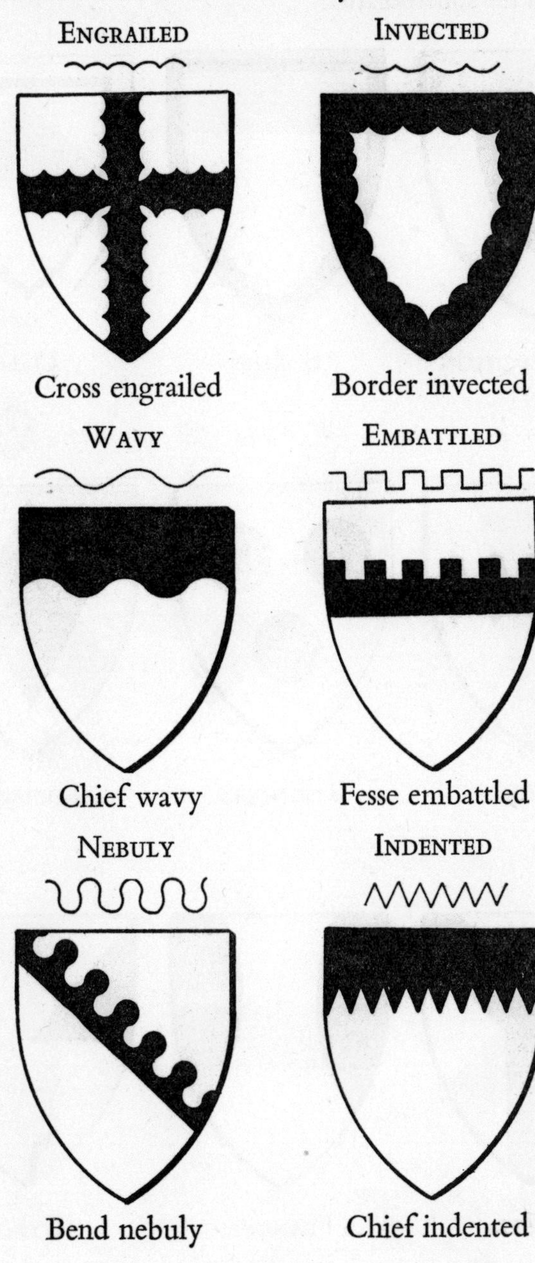

Some of the subordinaries:

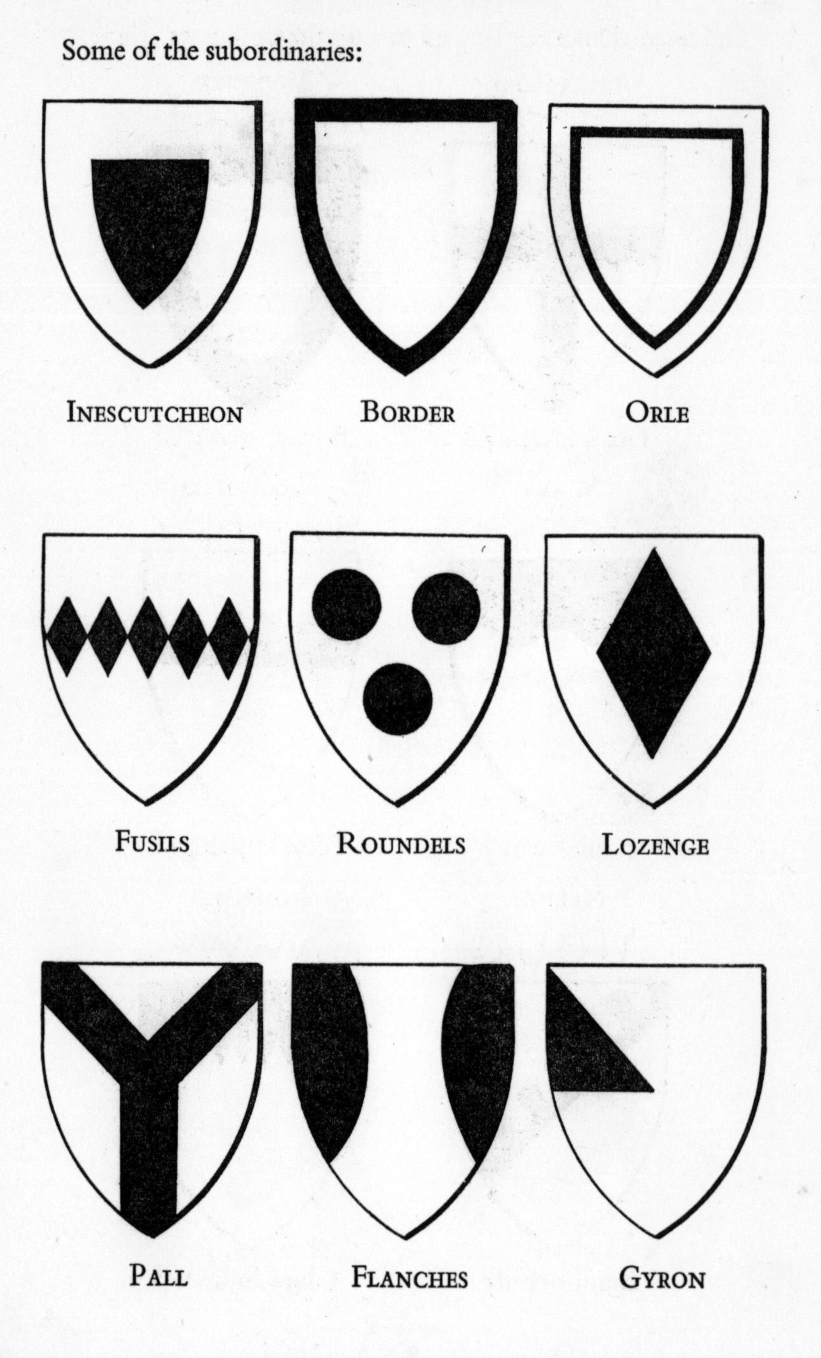

There are many varieties of the cross in heraldry. Here are some of them:

Cross couped

Cross (of) Calvary or Passion cross

Cross crosslet

Cross moline

Cross potent

Cross quarterly pierced

4

The Shield: More about Charges

ALMOST any common object could be, and has been, used as a charge in heraldry, though some of them have acquired different names: for instance, the 'garb,' one of the oldest charges, is really a sheaf of grain.

Among the miscellaneous objects which have played their part as designs upon a shield are the following:

SHELL
(scallop, escallop)

This originated as an heraldic emblem in the Crusades. Pilgrims used to hold out the shells for alms. It is now associated with travel.

WATER-BOUGET

A vessel to hold water, generally thought to have been introduced by Crusaders.

BEACON

An iron box containing fire on top of a high pole or tripod to which a ladder is fixed; sometimes called a 'Cresset.'

BRUSH
(fox's tail)

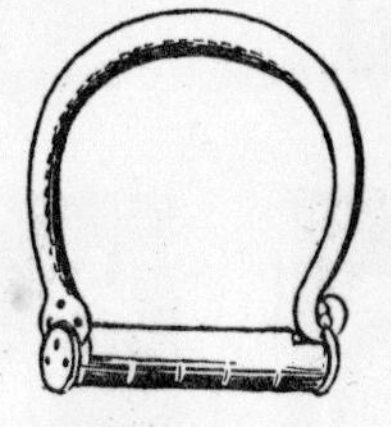

FETTERLOCK

A shackle and padlock resembling a handcuff, placed on prisoners' wrists and ankles.

BUGLE

Generally shown as hanging from two ribbons.

Then there are the flowers, trees, and plants which have contributed to our visual pleasure, as well as the birds, the fishes, and the animals—both real and legendary.

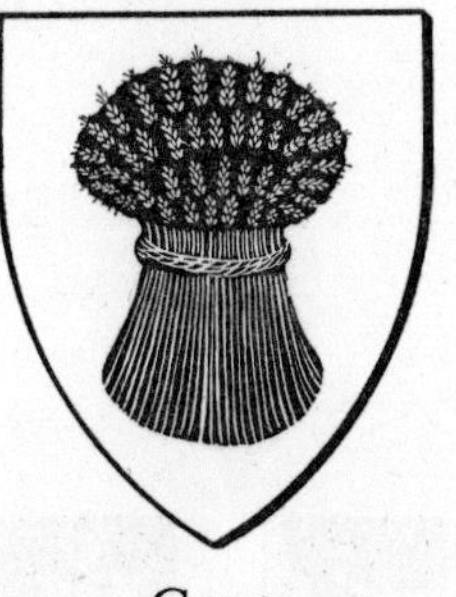

GARB

A sheaf of grain; unless otherwise stated, of wheat.

Among the animals in heraldry the lion takes first place. In the early days he just fitted into the shield as was most convenient. Then it came to be assumed that a lion meant a lion 'rampant' —*i.e.*, erect, with one hind-foot raised.

In olden times the lions in the Arms of England, which are 'passant guardant' (*i.e.*, walking with heads turned towards the spectator and with dexter paw raised), were always referred to as the leopards of England. The probable explanation is that in small drawings the old heraldic artists found it difficult to distinguish one from the other.

The lion's most usual positions are given below:

Rampant

Rampant guardant

Statant

Passant

Rampant reguardant

Sejant

Passant guardant

Couchant

The most important of the birds is the eagle. Birds with their wings spread out and the tips upward are said to be 'displayed'; if, however, the tips of the open wings are downward, as if the bird intended to alight or take off, it is said to be 'displayed and inverted.'

'Volant' means flying; and on the ground with wings closed is 'close.'

TWO TYPES OF HERALDIC EAGLES

Chief among heraldic monsters are the dragon—easily recognizable by its scales, the wyvern—resembling a dragon, but with only two legs, which are not unlike an eagle's, the griffin (gryphon), and the cockatrice—about which it is sufficient to say that it is supposed to have been evolved from a cock's egg hatched out by a serpent.

DRAGON WYVERN

GRIFFIN COCKATRICE

5

The Language of Heraldry: Blazoning

FIVE colours called 'tinctures' are used in heraldry; and as knights were decorating their shields in the days when kings of England had estates in France, and Norman-French was the language spoken at court, the colours were called by old French names. Red was 'gules'; blue, 'azure'; black (although it is not really a colour), 'sable'; green, 'vert'; and purple, 'purpure.' There are also two metals in use: gold, 'or'; and silver, 'argent'; some furs, of which the most important are 'ermine,' 'vair,' and —not so common—'potent.'

The heraldic artists seem to have known without being specifically told that it was best to paint shields in these five colours alone, and that if the field was silver or gold the charge should be in colour, and vice versa. This made for clarity (an essential on the battlefield), and resulted in combinations which could easily be seen at a distance.

This colour rule does not apply to a fur, or 'proper'—*i.e.*, any charge in its natural colour, since neither is a heraldic colour.

The accepted way of representing these tinctures in black and white is as follows:

(*a*) *or* shown by dots
(*b*) *argent* blank, or white
(*c*) *gules* vertical shading
(*d*) *azure* horizontal shading
(*e*) *sable* (*c*) and (*d*) combined
(*f*) *vert* diagonal shading, left down to right
(*g*) *purpure* diagonal shading, right down to left

These shadings are called 'hatchings.'

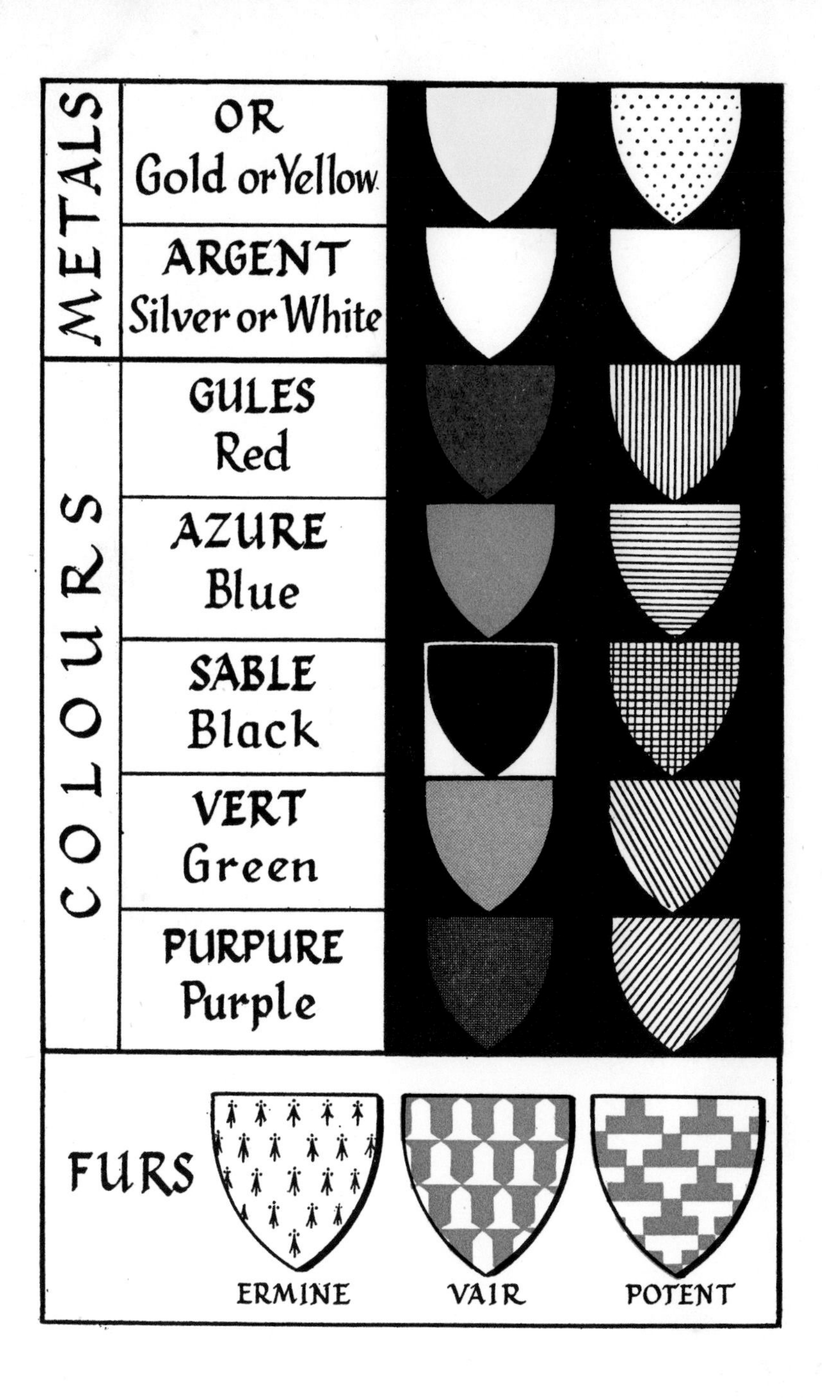

METALS, COLOURS, AND FURS

The rule that *metal should not be placed upon metal, nor colour upon colour*, was flouted in the case of the arms of Jerusalem, where five gold crosses are shown upon a silver field. This breach of the rule is understood to have been committed deliberately, in order that the arms of the Holy City might hold a unique position in the world of heraldry. The papal colours, gold and silver, were similarly chosen to honour the head of the Church.

Even when the need for quick identification in the field had ceased to exist, or at any rate had become less drastic, and shields were less clear-cut, this old rule was retained.

Blazoning

Arms consist of the devices, or charges, on a shield. If we describe them verbally we are said to 'blazon' the arms; but if we paint or colour them the process is known as '*em*blazoning.'

The verb 'to blazon,' in German (*blasen*), means to sound a trumpet; and when the knights of old entered the lists the Heralds 'blazoned' their arms—*i.e.*, they described their arms aloud, after a preliminary flourish of trumpets, hence the expression. The noun 'blazon' used to mean a shield, a coat-of-arms. The word now means the written description, in heraldic terms, of a coat-of-arms.

When blazoning a coat-of-arms we begin with a description of the field. On the Continent families sometimes have a coat-of-arms which consists of a plain uncharged field of one tincture—such as a plain golden shield, or a plain shield sable.

But no Englishman has ever borne a shield of one simple metal or colour, though it has been said that the Beringtons of Chester bore a plain blue shield; but this is not authentic.

One of the best ways to learn about heraldry is to get hold of some such book as a peerage, and examine the blazons. Afterwards test your knowledge by (*a*) trying to blazon arms from a picture, and (*b*) sketching arms from a blazon. Then check up to see just how right or wrong you are.

• • •

Let us examine the Shakespeare arms, a punning coat. It is a familiar coat, often used on bindings of Shakespeare's works, and it is carved on his monument at Stratford-on-Avon.

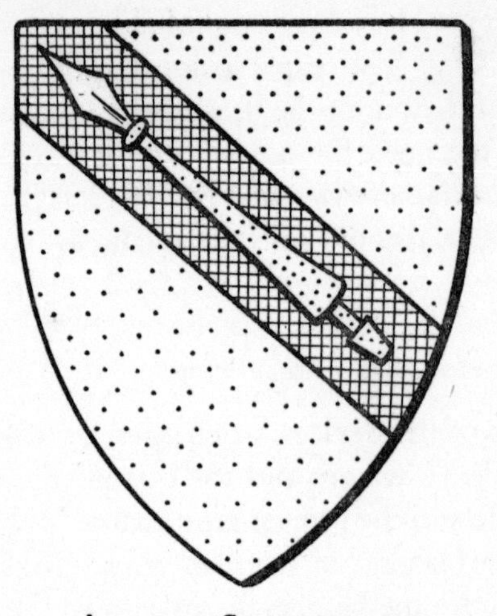

ARMS OF SHAKESPEARE

OR ON A BEND SABLE A SPEAR OF THE FIRST STEELED ARGENT

'*Or* . . .'

A blazon, as we have said, always begins with the colour, or tincture, of the field. The field here is or (gold), in our uncoloured illustration represented by dots (see page 28).

'*on a bend* . . .'

Having named the tincture of the field, the next step is to give the principal charge, the bend (one of the ordinaries), a broad diagonal band from the dexter chief to the sinister base—as illustrated on page 18.

'*sable* . . .'

The colour of the charge comes after the naming of the charge itself. Sable (black) is shown by a mixture of horizontal and vertical shading (see page 28).

'a spear . . .'

Spears and spear-heads were often used as charges, and unless otherwise stated the spear would be a tilting spear with a sharp head.

'of the first . . .'

In heraldry the name of a colour, or tincture, must not be used twice in the same blazon; so 'of the first' means of the first colour named, which is, in this example, or (gold).

If it had read 'of the second,' sable would be meant, as that is the second colour mentioned.

'steeled argent'

As the spear-head is of a different tincture (argent) to the shaft (or), it has to be mentioned in the blazon. 'Steeled' in heraldry means tipped, or headed, when speaking of weapons.

The use of canting arms accounted for a good many charges, but others stemmed from deeds of valour or from important events in the life of the bearer of the arms.

The Crusades proved a fruitful source, and to this great movement may be traced the numerous charges in the shape of a cross, though this does not mean that every cross implies a connexion with the Crusades.

Here are two examples of the cross as a charge:

(i) Le Brun
Azure a cross moline or (cross moline was illustrated on page 21).

(ii) John Wycliffe
Argent a chevron sable between three cross crosslets gules (cross crosslet and chevron were illustrated on pages 21 and 18 respectively.

The badge, the Red Hand of Ulster, commemorates a bloody deed, and, in a sense, a brave one, though at the back of it was greed for new territory.

Legend gives us the following to account for its adoption by the province of Ulster:

O'Neill, from whom the ancient kings of Ireland claimed descent, finding in a 'territorial' expedition to the coast of Ireland that a rival boat was gaining on his own, cut off his left hand at the landing and threw it on shore, so that he could claim that at least some part of him had been the first to touch the new territory.

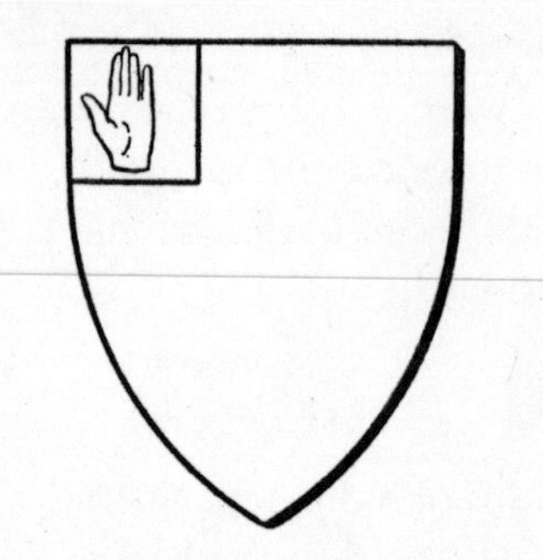

THE RED HAND
OF ULSTER

This badge is generally held to be a left hand 'appaumée' (open) upon a field argent.

But some authorities dispute this, saying that the badge of O'Neill was a right hand.

James I founded the order of baronets, hoping to make money by so doing, and he ordained that the open hand (dexter or sinister?) placed upon a 'canton,' or small square, in the corner of the shield, where it would not interfere with earlier armorial bearings, should be borne by the baronets of the united kingdoms.

A Modern Coat

The arms of the British Broadcasting Corporation, granted and assigned to them under Letters Patent dated the 8th day of March 1927:

ARMS. *Azure, a terrestrial globe proper encircled by an annulet or, and seven estoiles, in orle argent.*

CREST. *On a wreath of the colours a lion passant or grasping in the dexter forepaw a thunderbolt proper.*

SUPPORTERS. *On either side an eagle, wings addorsed* (back to back)—*proper collared azure pendant therefrom a bugle horn stringed or.*

BADGE. *A thunderbolt proper thereon a pellet inscribed with the letters B.B.C. in gold.*

MOTTO. *Nation shall speak peace unto nation.*

ARMS OF THE
BRITISH BROADCASTING CORPORATION

6

Helmets, Mantling, Wreaths, Crests, Crowns, Coronets, Mitres

GENERALLY the word 'arms' in heraldry means the shield itself with its charges, and does not include the other articles of the achievement.

Helmets

First to be considered among these is the helmet. This is usually shown on top of the shield. But peers have the coronet of their rank resting on the shield and the helmet on top of that.

One of the lessons taught to students of heraldry was that the helmet, by its shape and position, gave an indication of the wearer's rank. The formula was: king and princes—of gold, 'affrontée' (facing the spectator) with six or seven bars across the front; peer—of silver, with five gold bars, in profile; baronet or knight—of silver, with a visor either open or closed, affrontée; esquire—of silver, closed.

But these rules are not part of what may be called the 'old' heraldry. They came into existence in the time of the Stuarts, when heraldry was in a state of decline; and they were really for the convenience of a new race of heraldic artists, who lacked the knowledge of the old ones, and had to have a pattern to go by.

More than ever, perhaps, in our semi-hatless age, does one tend to wonder how the knights of old managed to carry on their heads a helmet with a wooden or leather crest on top of that. The fact was that they did not wear them continuously. The helmets were slung at the saddle bow until the time for the actual knocking

Helmets:

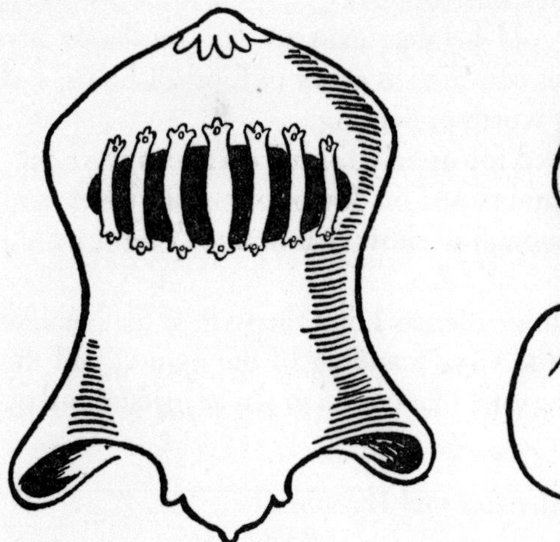

King and princes

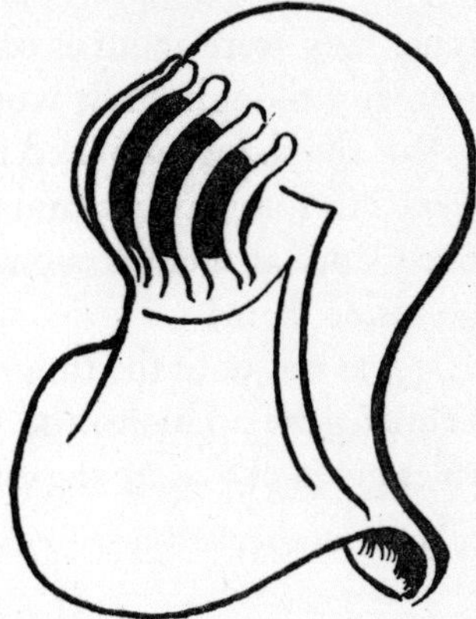

Peer

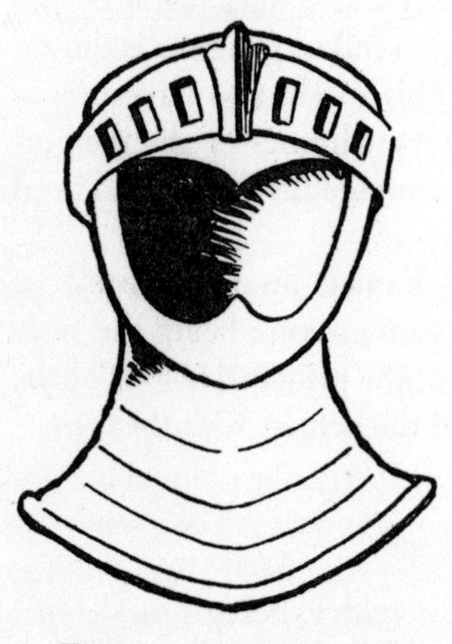

Baronet or knight

Esquire

about drew near, and they were so made that when worn the weight rested on the shoulders. For ceremonial occasions the helmet was carried by a page until needed.

Very few genuinely old helmets exist to-day—probably because they were about as common as a pair of football-boots, and were not thought to be worth preserving.

But the sham ones used for merely formal occasions were preserved to some extent, and passed on down to modern times; and one glance at them is enough to show that nobody's head would go inside them!

It was not until the time of James I that the style of the heraldic helmet gave a clue to the social standing of the owner; and the rules given above are the ones that obtain in Great Britain to-day.

Mantling and Wreaths

Mantling (lambrequin) was the name given to the flowing drapery which you see attached to the helmet and gracefully displayed round the shield. It was intended to remind people of the veiling worn by the Crusaders to protect them, and also their helmets, from the hot sun of Palestine.

In the coat-of-arms the mantling was so arranged that it showed scalloped edges, reminiscent of the cuts and slashes made by the weapons of the enemy, these forming a kind of fringe as is shown in the frontispiece. This might also have been a way of reminding stay-at-homes of the dangers to which their more courageous friends had been exposed.

WREATH (torse)

The wreath (torse) is made up of two bands of silk interwoven and twisted, one being the tincture of the principal metal, the other of the principal colour of the arms. It was used to conceal the join of the helmet with the crest.

Crests and Wreaths

The crest existed before the days of heraldry, being a model of a bird or beast, inanimate object or part of the human body, placed

CREST

upon the helmet, its purpose being to serve as a decoration, and also to break the force of a downward blow upon the head.

Later on it was often a figure taken from the arms: but, though arms could be had without a crest, a crest could not be had without arms, as some folks still seem to think.

There are many people who call a family coat-of-arms, or the school coat, a crest—forgetting that the crest is merely the device which surmounts the helmet.

The crest may have had its uses as a rallying-point on the battlefield, but it is difficult to believe that some of the cumbrous objects to be found in illustrations ever appeared in actual warfare, though they may have done in tournaments.

The early crests were painted on metal, which was then placed on the helmet; later carved on wood or made in boiled leather (*cuir bouilli*), which stood up well to the weather. The 'chapeau,' or 'cap of dignity,' or 'cap of maintenance,' at one time worn only by important persons but now borne regardless of rank, is then used to support the crest instead of a wreath. (In that form it could be used as a charge.) The chapeau, unless otherwise blazoned, is assumed to be gules and ermine.

Crowns, Coronets, and Mitres

The war helms of kings and princes were adorned with crowns so that they might be recognized by everybody—friend and enemy alike.

Crowns and coronets are exclusively the headgear of kings, princes, and peers. A crown, as distinguished from a coronet, has bars arched over the top.

We owe the arched Royal Crown to Henry V, and a carved scene over his chantry in Westminster Abbey shows his coronation with this type of crown.

Until Elizabeth II adopted the bowed arched crown the heraldic crown had not changed since the end of Victoria's reign.

ROYAL CROWN
(Tudor type)

ROYAL CROWN
(Modern type)

The coronet of the Prince of Wales is like the Royal Crown, but with one arched bar instead of two.

There are numbers of coronets in actual use at coronation ceremonies as well as in heraldry, where they are worn by children of the Sovereign, by dukes, marquesses, earls, viscounts, barons.

The younger children of the Sovereign wear coronets of the same pattern as the Heir Apparent's, but without arches.

Grandchildren of the Sovereign descended from sons in the direct line show strawberry leaves instead of two of the crosses patée.

THE SOVEREIGN'S YOUNGER CHILDREN

DUKE

MARQUESS

The heraldic version of a duke's coronet carries eight gold strawberry leaves (five showing), that of a marquess, four gold strawberry leaves alternating with four silver balls (of which three leaves and two balls are seen in representation). The silver balls on

EARL VISCOUNT BARON

coronets are often spoken of as pearls, though imitation pearls are banned for this purpose.

An earl on his coronet has eight pearls (five showing) raised on points, with a leaf between each pair of points. A viscount has nine pearls showing, while a baron has a plain silver-gilt circlet with six large silver balls, of which only four are to be seen.

All these coronets are usually worn about a crimson cap with a gold tassel; but this may be omitted in representations and in actual use. At the coronation of King George VI the Princesses Elizabeth and Margaret Rose wore their coronets without caps.

Of the special forms of crown, the 'Mural Crown' is the most frequent, and is to be seen on civic arms. A variation of it is to be seen above the arms of the London County Council. The mural crown was at one time granted, though infrequently, to famous soldiers. It is masoned and embattled—*i.e.*, showing stonework of a building and battlements of towers or churches.

MURAL CROWN ASTRAL CROWN NAVAL CROWN

The 'Astral Crown,' awarded to distinguished members of the Air Force, is a circlet on which are mounted four stars (three only visible), each star being placed between a pair of elevated wings.

The 'Naval Crown' was similarly granted to distinguished sailors. This is a circlet on which appear the sterns and sails of ships alternately. It is part of the insignia of the naval towns of Chatham and Plymouth.

The arms of archbishops and bishops are surmounted by a mitre instead of a helmet. The Bishopric of Durham, however, was, until the beginning of the last century, a Palatinate—*i.e.*, the province of one enjoying Royal privileges.

Therefore in this case the mitre which surmounts the arms is placed within a ducal coronet.

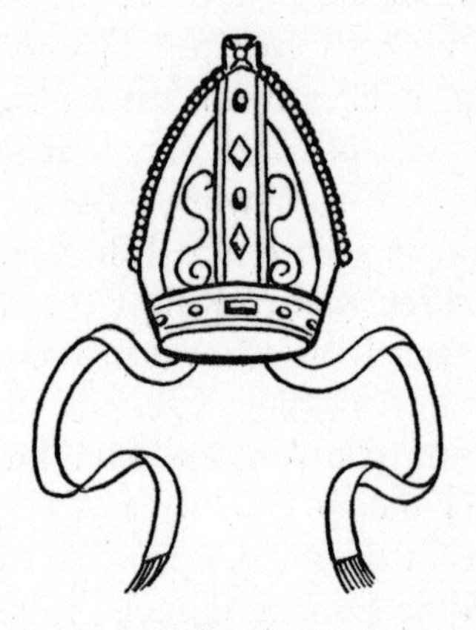

MITRE

7

Mottoes and Supporters: Badges

THE MOTTO is usually to be found on a scroll under the achievement. Quite frequently this was a survival of the war-cry of the bearer of the arms or of one of his ancestors, and there was nothing permanent about it. A motto could be changed at any time if the bearer of the arms thought of a better one.

The Royal Family, peers, a number of persons honoured by the Sovereign—such as Knights of the Garter and Thistle, Knights Grand Cross of other orders and corporate bodies—may display 'supporters.' These are the birds, animals, human beings, or angels which are placed on either side of the shield, as if 'supporting' it.

Probably the spaces between the flanks of the shield and the motto which went round them offended the feeling for design of the old-time engravers of seals, who filled them up in this way—just as earlier they had decorated the background by adding the mantling to the helmet. And since the supporters, unless they are given a foothold of some kind, would appear to be dangling in mid-air, they are provided with a 'compartment,' which may be either land or sea, or, among other things, the motto scroll.

In passing it may be noted with interest that supporters of the Royal Arms were first, but infrequently, used in the reign of Richard II; though Edward III had sometimes made use of a golden lion and a silver falcon. Richard II's first supporters were two angels, supporting the shield, and below the shield was a white hart—a very favourite badge of this king's. The supporters best known to us are the Lion and the Unicorn as shown in the Royal Arms (see frontispiece).

Badges

The 'badge' is an emblem associated with the achievement, though not actually part of it. It was not necessarily hereditary, and a man might have several badges if he so chose.

Badges, an important feature of heraldry, particularly in the reign of Edward III, were devices displayed as the distinguishing mark of a man on standards and liveries. Though, as has been stated, a badge was not part of the achievement like the crest, it was often something taken from the arms. Badges were displayed by the families to whom they belonged, and were worn by their retainers, also by the owner's followers, personal friends, and admirers who wished to take his side in the event of a quarrel.

THE BEAR AND THE RAGGED STAFF

One of the most famous badges of all time, a common sight in England during the Wars of the Roses, was the Bear and the Ragged Staff of the Earl of Warwick, appropriately nicknamed 'The Kingmaker.' (Incidentally, Warwick acquired this badge from his heiress-wife. It now figures in the arms of the Warwickshire County Council and as the cap-badge of the Warwickshire Yeomanry.)

The Earl of Warwick, like other powerful figures in history, had a way of amassing hordes of followers in one part or another of the countryside, in readiness to pick a quarrel on the flimsiest of excuses with another set of men wearing a different badge.

Well-known badges to-day are the Rose, the Thistle, and the Shamrock, the first-named being the most famous of all English Royal badges. The first rose was a golden one, brought from Provence by Eleanor, Henry III's queen. It remained a Royal badge until the death of Richard II in 1399, when the Lancastrians succeeded, and brought their own red rose to the English throne. The white rose was a badge of the next dynasty, the House of York.

ROYAL BADGES

ROSE THISTLE SHAMROCK

When, in 1485, Henry VII came to the throne and married Princess Elizabeth of York, the red and the white roses were united, giving us the Tudor Rose as we know it to-day.

Hardly less well known is the Leek, the badge of Wales.

Widely used throughout the Commonwealth as a badge is the Crown itself, as well as the Sovereign's crowned initials—the Royal Cipher.

The Civil Service and other employees of the Crown make use, in the Sovereign's name, of the Royal Arms and Badges: the Yeomen Warders of the Tower still wear the Rose, the Thistle, etc., on breast and back in medieval style; while the State Trumpeters show the Royal Cipher on their gold-and-crimson tunics.

The Bear and the Ragged Staff appears, we said, as the cap-badge of the Warwickshire Yeomanry; another famous badge, the Portcullis (brought into the Tudor family by Lady Margaret Beaufort, the mother of Henry Tudor, afterwards Henry VII), is displayed by the Royal Gloucestershire Hussars, and is part of the Queen's Westminsters' (The King's Royal Rifle Corps) badge. It represents a grating which could be lowered in the defence of a gateway, or raised at will.

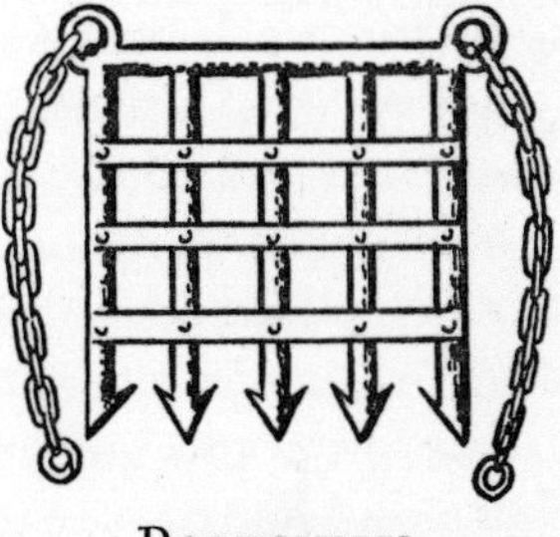

PORTCULLIS

8

Marshalling: Differencing and Cadency Marks

MARSHALLING is the grouping together in one composition of two or more coats-of-arms. This can be done in three different ways: 'dimidiation,' 'impalement,' and 'quartering.'

Dimidiation was the oldest method used. It consisted in placing the sinister half of the wife's coat-of-arms beside the dexter half of the husband's. In the process the appearance of both coats was spoiled. The most famous example of dimidiation occurs in the arms of the Cinque Ports, where the foreparts of the three lions passant guardant of England are joined to the stern ends of three ships.

Not quite so famous, but even funnier, are the arms of Great Yarmouth, where the foreparts of the three lions passant are joined to the rear halves of three herrings.

Dimidiation, being found to be unsatisfactory, had only a short life, dying out towards the end of the fourteenth century to make room for impalement, or impaling.

In this method, which is still in use, the husband's and the wife's coats are placed side by side within the compass of the shield.

So, if a man marries a woman who has a right to bear arms, her arms are placed beside his on the shield; but their children, if they have any, would inherit their father's arms only.

Last of all came quartering, in which the shield is divided into four or more parts, according to the number of coats-of-arms to be displayed; there being a complete coat in each section.

If there are only two coats the most important is displayed in the first and fourth quarters, and the other in the second and third.

HOW A MEDIEVAL KNIGHT AND HIS FAMILY DISPLAYED THEIR ARMS
(From the Luttrell Psalter)

If three the most important one still has priority claim on the first and fourth quarters, the other two being placed on the second and third respectively.

The reason for the repeat of a coat is the existence in heraldry of the rule which requires that no quarter shall be left blank.

The need for the marshalling of several coats-of-arms on a shield arises from marriages to heraldic 'heiresses': and here, to prevent confusion, it must be explained that in heraldry an heiress does not mean a woman who possesses a title, landed estates, a large income, pearls and diamonds, or town and country houses.

A heraldic heiress is one who, when her father dies (he being armigerous) has no brothers, and so inherits her father's arms, with the right to transmit them to her children, should she have any. If she has sisters they become co-heiresses, with the same rights.

But—if she has a brother who dies before his father, leaving a daughter, that daughter, and not her aunts, becomes the heiress of the arms.

When an heiress marries her arms, instead of being placed alongside her husband's by impalement, are displayed on a small shield on the middle of her husband's shield. This is called an 'escutcheon of pretence.'

Children of such a marriage have the right to bear their father's arms in the first and fourth quarters, with their mother's coat in the second and third.

Several generations of marriages with heiresses may result in a large number of quarterings being brought into the family arms; but if the number is above four, the four quarters of the shield may become 'grand quarters,' one or more being sub-divided to take the extra coats.

At this point you may well be saying, "This has gone far enough."

But now apply the rulings to real people, and it may seem less complicated:

Mr Wilson, let us say, marries Miss Robinson. But as either of the couple would be too big to go into one of our miniature shields, Mr Wilson shall be A and Miss Robinson B.

A marries a non-heiress, who, however, has the right to bear arms B (note the lozenge), and her arms are impaled alongside his A B. (Remember, though, that their children would not have the right to use B.)

If, on the other hand, B was an heiress the married coat-of-arms would be A B, and their children would bear A B B A. Now things are beginning to get a little more involved.

Suppose that A and B have a son who marries an heiress with a plain (*i.e.* not quartered) coat-of-arms, the married coat would be

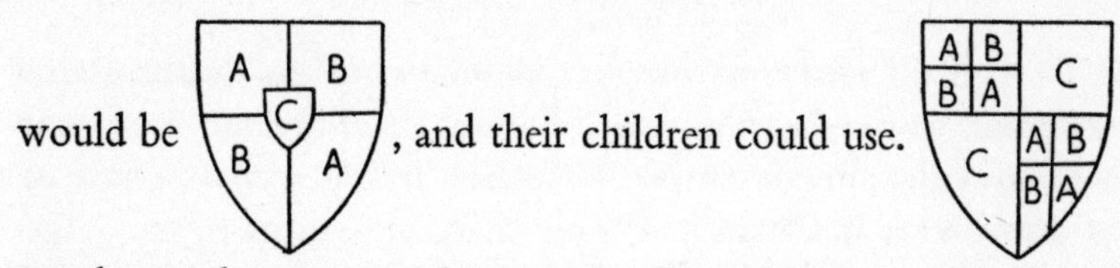

, and their children could use.

But he might marry an heiress who herself has a quartered coat and any children of *this* marriage would bear arms . Thus each grand quarter would itself be quartered, and as time passed, bringing with it further developments, the situation would become even more complicated.

Some one in Tudor times must have thought so at any rate; for in that period it was decided to ignore the custom of dividing into four each time, and coats began to be added consecutively, shields becoming

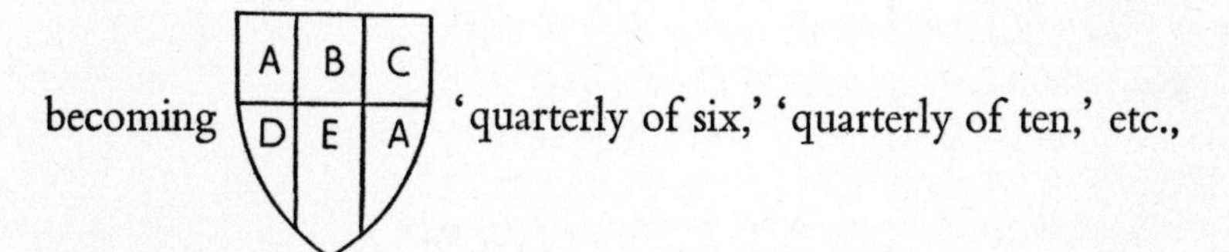

'quarterly of six,' 'quarterly of ten,' etc., any odd quarter at the end being filled with a repeat of the most important arms. This lessened the congestion a little.

Moreover, families of the ancient nobility formed the habit of selecting some of the more important inherited coats, throwing out a few heiresses here and there by the way if the quarterings threatened to become too numerous.

And any layman struggling to sort out his family tree, if he got

into difficulties, could always appeal to the College of Arms for some one to step in and give him advice.

Differencing and Cadency Marks

Though no two men might wear the same coat-of-arms, an exception was made in the case of members of one family. But it became evident in due course that such an arrangement might have its drawbacks. If a man had more than one son of fighting age considerable confusion might arise if father and son were buried in armour and had identical charges on their shields.

So there arose the system of cadency marks to do with the descent of the younger branches; and in our own country, since Tudor days, there has existed the custom of 'differencing' the coats-of-arms of the sons in a family, each having his own special mark.

The eldest has his 'label' (file), which he drops when his father dies and he succeeds to the family coat.

A label can be represented by a piece of silk or linen with three 'pendants.'

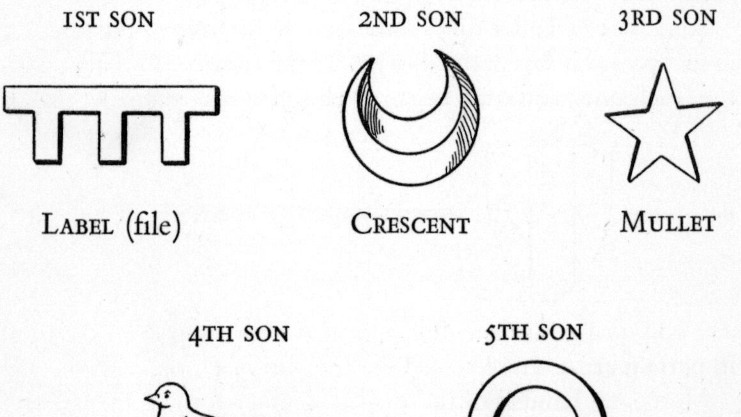

MARTLET

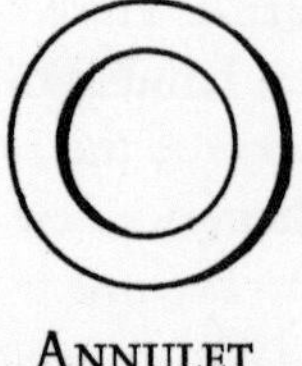

ANNULET

Probably the above number would be enough; but if there were more sons in the family the list continued as follows: for the sixth son, a fleur-de-lis; for the seventh, a rose; for the eighth, a cross moline; and for the ninth (probably the baby in his cradle), an eight-petalled flower. (He might have it embroidered on his bib, if he had one.)

The colour rule is relaxed in the case of cadency marks. They may be of any heraldic tincture.

Our most famous eldest son is Charles, Prince of Wales, Heir Apparent to the Throne, automatically Duke of Cornwall in England by descent from the Plantagenets. (The Black Prince was the first Duke of Cornwall.)

Prince Charles differences the Royal Arms with a plain white label, the emblem of the Heir Apparent to the throne. As Prince of Wales he also includes the arms of Wales and his special coronet with one arched bar.

9

Seals and Banners: Corporate Heraldry

Seals

THE collecting of seals might well claim to be the oldest hobby in the world, for it became the fashion in ancient Rome, Julius Caesar himself being a devotee.

In Babylon and China, too, people of importance possessed and used these fascinating objects. Early in the history of civilization, we learn that everybody who was anybody had his own seal, which was, in effect, his signature.

The study of seals has contributed a great deal to the knowledge of medieval heraldry, for they show knights on horseback, and arms on shields, on surcoats, and trappers.

The present series of the Great Seals of the English Monarchy starts with the authentic seal of Edward the Confessor (1043).

The obverse shows the King on the throne holding sceptre and orb. On the reverse he is also seen upon the throne, but here he holds a sceptre (surmounted by a dove of peace and mercy) in one hand, and the sword of justice in the other.

Among the sovereigns who reigned between Edward the Confessor and Elizabeth II, the one who was most partial to seals was probably Edward III, who had eight Great Seals during his reign.

This may have been partly due to the fact that his reign was a long one (1327–77), and he needed a change now and then; perhaps also to the circumstance that the fourteenth century was a good period for the engraver's art, when a skilled craftsman could be sure of a steady run of customers, even among royalties.

But not only royal customers. When writing was an accomplishment looked upon with contempt as being only fit for monks, and a seal did all that was really necessary, it behoved every 'gentleman' to possess one.

The Stuart King, James II, threw his Great Seal into the Thames when he fled from the country in 1688, hoping to make things awkward for his successor; but, luckily for William the Dutchman, a fisherman pulled it out of the river a few days later. He must have thought it rather an unusual catch.

In our own country, on the death of the Sovereign, the old seal is used until the new Sovereign orders otherwise.

Then the old seal, defaced to render it unfit for use, is by custom presented to the Lord Chancellor, who is also Keeper of the Great Seal. Elizabeth II observed this custom on August 2, 1953, two months after her Coronation.

The new Great Seal, on the obverse of which is a portrait of the Queen on horseback, wearing the uniform of Colonel-in-Chief, Grenadier Guards, was designed by Mr Gilbert Ledward R.A., and engraved in silver at the Royal Mint. It weighs 135 ounces and has a diameter of six inches.

SEAL OF THE COUNTY PALATINE OF LANCASTER

On the obverse side of the new County Palatine of Lancaster Seal the Queen is shown in uniform, mounted on the police-horse Winston, with one of her corgis running beside Winston's foreleg.

The designer of this seal admitted that he had taken some liberties in his designs, for though the Queen is dressed as for Trooping the Colour, she carries the sceptre in her right hand.

Rose-bushes form the background, and the Lancastrian badge, a rose surmounted by a crown, is shown.

The Pennon, the Banner, the Standard

The three names above represent the flags of the Middle Ages.

The pennon, carried by knights, was narrow and triangular in shape, either pointed or swallow-tailed at the free end. It was charged with the owner's arms, badge, and sometimes other heraldic devices, and was borne by him on his lance as his personal flag.

The banner was a larger flag, which might be either square or rectangular. It bore the owner's arms emblazoned on its entire surface as if it were a shield, the dexter side being considered to be the one nearest the flagstaff. If the banner is viewed with the staff on the right it should always be remembered that the arms will be viewed reversed, left to right.

It did not, however, bear the helm, crest, or any other accessories of the shield.

It was the ensign of the Sovereign, princes, peers, or a knight banneret—*i.e.*, a knight promoted on the battlefield "for valour." When this happened to him a ceremony was performed on the spot, the pointed end of his pennon being cut off, thus transforming it into the shape of a small banner.

No one below the rank of a knight banneret might carry a banner.

The banner of the Sovereign in early times, if the regulations were complied with, was five feet square. That of a duke was four feet, and the banners of other nobles a mere three feet square.

EARLY HERALDIC BANNERS

HOW A CHARGE LOOKS ON EITHER SIDE OF A BANNER

Measurements must have varied a little for those banners which were rectangular without being square.

The standard was a much bigger flag than the banner, its proportions varying according to the rank of the owners. The standard of the Sovereign was eight yards long, the knight's a beggarly four. The standard, instead of being carried, was stuck in the soil, and from there the owner used it as a rallying point for his followers.

HERALDIC STANDARD

Unlike the banner, the standard was not armorial. Next to the staff there usually appeared in olden times the Cross of St George on a white ground; the rest of the standard was of the colours of the livery. The 'livery' was worn by the servants of the owner of the arms.

Livery colours were not necessarily confined to tinctures of arms. One of the Lancastrian colours was murrey (a reddish purple). The Tudors used green and white, which do not appear on their shield.

Upon this portion of the standard were depicted the badges and sometimes the crest of the owner.

The esquires, at the other end of the scale, carried a triangular-shaped pennon called a 'penoncel,' or pensil. These flags have their descendants in the pennons which were flown on the cars of commanders in the army, charged with formation badges. Graded in a descending order of importance according to the rank of the commander, they are rectangular, swallow-tailed, triangular.

At sea the sails of ships were often emblazoned with arms, and the pennon became a long, whiplike flag. This is still used. It is pronounced as 'pennant' and spelt p-e-n-d-a-n-t.

Corporate Heraldry

The first sign of corporate arms may be said to have appeared when Richard I's lions became part of the Royal Arms of England. This event may have happened as a result of the immense prestige of the Lionheart, who left a trail of glamour wherever he went; but more probably it was one of the outward and visible signs of a change in the minds of men themselves.

Not only had the Crusades (1095–1291), which gave a tremendous fillip to heraldry, engendered an almost worshipful attitude to arms, but the old idea of every man for himself was losing ground.

The Crusaders were bound together in a common cause: was some curious kind of alchemy working secretly in the minds of mankind, so that the general good was becoming more important than the welfare of the individual?

May it not have been some such reasoning (perhaps subconscious) that gave succeeding dynasties the idea of adopting what had been hitherto a personal emblem as part of the Royal Arms of England—thus linking the Sovereign with his subjects?

Arms spread to institutions. No longer were they the prerogative of powerful knights and barons and princes of the Church, but they were assumed by abbeys, monasteries, cities. Trade associations, stemming from the old guilds, became great Livery Companies, with their own arms.

The origins of corporate arms are not always easy to trace. Some have a legendary basis, sometimes they were the personal arms of a founder or donor, and others were granted by Charter.

Such things as the airscrew in the Hendon crest and the locomotive on the Swindon shield are evidence of the impact of heraldry on modern life. As an example of its widespread use by the institutions and companies in this country, on page 56 is an illustration of the Arms of the Institution of Electrical Engineers.

The City of Birmingham, interested in the arts, has linked old and new in an unusual manner; for while her shield displays the arms of the de Berminghams (ancient Lords of the Manor), the supporters are figures designed to represent respectively engineering and art.

Arms of the
Institute of Electrical Engineers

Blazon: Azure, within an annulet florettée at the four cardinal points a winged thunderbolt or; on a chief barry wavy azure and or, an open book proper garnished gules, on the leaves thereof the words "DISCE DOCE" in letters sable. And for the crest, on a wreath of the colours a leopard statant or supporting in his dexter forepaw a caduceus of the same; as supporters, on a compartment vert, two pegasi argent, crined, hoofed, and winged or, each charged on the breast with a St Michael's cross gules.

10

Royal Heraldry: The Queen's Beasts

PART ONE

HERALDRY itself is hardly older than the Royal Arms of England, which first appear on the second Great Seal of Richard Coeur de Lion—the first seal to include a coat-of-arms. The first Great Seal was lost at sea.

Elizabeth II of England is a descendant of the sovereigns of England and of the ancient kings of Scotland. She therefore quarters the coats of these kingdoms. They are her exclusive property and may not be used without her permission.

The quarterly coat is flown to mark the Queen's presence on shore or at sea, and is known as the Royal Standard. This, nevertheless, is incorrect, for a standard narrows to the point, which the Royal 'Standard' does not. The Royal Banner would be a better name.

The Duke of Edinburgh belongs to the same Royal Family as the kings of Denmark, Greece, and Norway. With the Royal Arms of Denmark and Greece (his father's family), the Duke quarters the arms of Mountbatten (his mother's family) and also those of the royal City of Edinburgh, from which his title derives. (The castle is, of course, a heraldic one, and not Edinburgh Castle itself.)

For many centuries now all members of the Royal Family have had differenced versions of the Royal Arms settled on them by Royal Warrant. On their white labels (three points for the

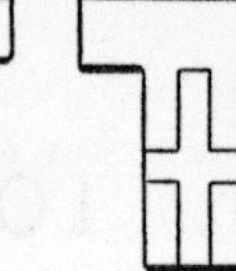
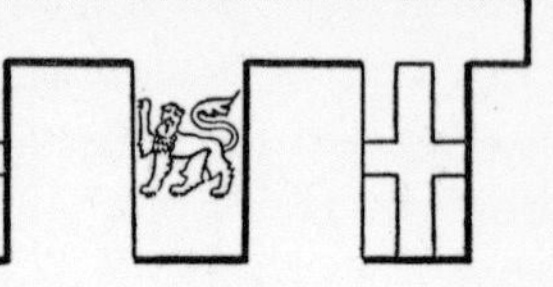

LABEL OF H.R.H. THE PRINCESS MARGARET

LABEL OF H.R.H. THE DUKE OF GLOUCESTER

Sovereign's children, five points for grandchildren) each prince or princess has individual marks as his or her particular difference. Princess Margaret, for instance, shows a thistle centre and two Tudor Roses at the sides. The Duke of Gloucester shows a lion centre and two crosses at the sides.

Princess Margaret's arms are displayed on a lozenge.

THE QUEEN'S BEASTS

I. The Lion of England
II. The Griffin of Edward III
III. The Falcon of the Plantagenets
IV. The Black Bull of Clarence
V. The White Lion of Mortimer
VI. The Yale of Beaufort
VII. The White Greyhound of Richmond
VIII. The Red Dragon of Wales
IX. The Unicorn of Scotland
X. The White Horse of Hanover

Among the most notable of the decorations designed in honour of the Coronation of Queen Elizabeth II in June 1953 were the ten heraldic beasts set up outside the great window of the Annexe to the Abbey shortly before Coronation Day.

These ten beasts had points in common: each rose to a full six feet high; each held a shield of arms; and—more important—each was in some way connected with the Queen's ancestry.

Crowds of sightseers looked at them and admired them; but perhaps because there were so many other attractions in London at the time of the Coronation, the Beasts received less attention than they deserved. Moreover, though many people had read the printed descriptions of them that were to be had, there were also a great many who had not done so, and in the minds of these there existed some confusion as to whether or no the Beasts actually belonged to the Queen, whether they had any connexion with those at Hampton Court Palace, and whether they were old or new.

The facts are that they belong to the Queen, and the ten set up at Westminster were chosen out of about thirty that she inherited, to be part of the Coronation decorations.

They were specially designed for the occasion, yet they derived from heraldic animals to be seen at Hampton Court Palace, which themselves derive from the ones made for King Henry VIII more than four hundred years ago.

The peak time for the Beasts vogue was in the fifteenth and sixteenth centuries, the fashion spreading from royalties down to plain knights, each of whom had his Beast, perhaps more than one, which guarded his house either inside or out.

Royal Beasts were to be seen all over the country, particularly in the palaces, in many parts of Windsor Castle, and in St George's Chapel, where several of them to this day seem to be having fun on the canopy of the royal pew, on the north side of the chancel. There are a large number on the roof of the Chapel as well.

Henry VIII's Beasts, at Hampton Court, included ten leopards with crowns about their necks for Anne Boleyn.

When Anne fell from grace, however, and was beheaded in 1536 Henry, practising economy, saw that with new heads and tails the leopards could be made over into ten panthers for Jane Seymour. This was accordingly done, and the new Queen's arms and badges were added. Time passed, and William III, living there at a later date, threw all the Beasts into the moat and had the moat filled in.

But years later, in 1909, the moat was cleared, and enough of the Beasts were exhumed to serve as a guide for the design of those which stand on the parapet of the bridge to-day; and those were the ones that inspired the new series which formed part of the 1953 Coronation decorations.

The ten Beasts were positioned outside the Abbey as they best fitted into the surroundings, without reference to length of pedigree as royal possessions, the Lion of England being first, as was its right.

It was thought desirable that they should be of neutral shades against the Abbey background; so, though the shields they held were coloured, the Beasts themselves were not.

I. *The Lion of England*

Pride of place given to the Lion of England at Westminster was most fittingly bestowed, for of all the Beasts placed outside the Abbey, was he not the King—the only one to wear a crown? And had he not been 'in' on such functions as coronations and royal weddings since the year 1127, when he adorned the cap and shoes of bridegroom Geoffrey Plantagenet, Count of Anjou and Maine, at his wedding with Princess Maud, daughter of King Henry I, who gave his son-in-law a blue shield powdered with little golden lions—the first coat-of-arms that we really know anything about?

And from that marriage all English kings and queens, from Henry II to Elizabeth II, are descended.

Perhaps Henry I used the lion as a personal device; but it was Henry II's son, Richard the Lionheart, who first displayed, as the Royal Arms, three golden lions set one above the other in a red field.

The Lion of England has appeared in many different places: on the crest of Richard I; on the Great Seal of Henry III; on flags flown by a sovereign's ships; carved in stone; painted on glass; embroidered on hangings; worked in wool; photographed as often as a film star.

At Westminster the English Lion held a shield of the Royal Arms as borne since Queen Victoria's accession, in 1837. The shield is divided into four quarters, with the lions of England in the first and fourth, the lion and tressure of Scotland in the second, and the Irish harp in the third.

II. *The Griffin of Edward III*

A model of this creature, said to be over three thousand years old, shows it with the head and wings of an eagle, but with the body, all four legs, and tail of a lion. But in heraldry it appears with the forelegs and claws also changed to those of an eagle, and with pointed ears added. So we meet an old friend here, for this is how Tenniel drew the Gryphon (Griffin) for *Alice's Adventures in Wonderland*.

Edward III had many beasts, but (after the Lion of England) his favourites were the griffin and the falcon; and of these two the griffin came first. He even had it on his private seal.

Naturally, then, these were the beasts chosen to represent him at Westminster; for represented he had to be, seeing that two of his sons founded the royal houses of Lancaster and York, whose union after many years of fighting resulted in the dynasty of Tudor.

You may take your choice of the legends which surround the griffin: (*a*) it was sacred to the sun; (*b*) it guarded a treasure in the East; (*c*) it would never be taken alive, preferring death to captivity; (*d*) it was violently allergic to horses; (*e*) it was so strong that it could carry off a man in full armour (horse and all) or even a couple of yoked oxen.

Yet the strange thing is that the winged griffin, which is the one shown in heraldry, is the female of the species.

At Westminster the Queen's Griffin displayed the badge of the present Royal House of Windsor: the Round Tower of Windsor Castle with the Royal Standard flying from the Tower. The Tower is enclosed by two branches of oak, and at the top is the arched Royal Crown. This was charged on a shield of red and gold, the colours of the present Royal Livery.

III. *The Falcon of the Plantagenets*

Although at Westminster the falcon was chosen, like the griffin, to represent Edward III, it was also closely associated with his great-great-grandson, Edward IV, and the shield the falcon holds is charged with one of Edward IV's badges, the falcon-and-fetterlock (this is really *two* badges). The shield itself is of the livery colours of the House of York, mulberry and blue.

Here the silver falcon stands within an open golden fetterlock, which to-day might be called a padlock. The bird has a slightly

THE LION OF ENGLAND

THE GRIFFIN OF EDWARD III

defiant look, and rather resembles a venturesome schoolboy, with feet planted apart, who is trying to keep his balance on the roller while at the same time the groundsman rolls the cricket pitch.

Edward III loved hawking, which explains his adoption of the falcon, and he named one of his Kings of Arms "Falcon."

Members of his family also used the bird, in particular his grandson and successor Richard II, who once appeared at a tournament at Windsor with an escort of forty knights and forty esquires dressed in green with white falcons.

When Edward IV became King he ordered his younger son Richard, Duke of York, to take as his badge a white falcon perched in a gold fetterlock, the lock being slightly open to show that his father had forced the lock and gained the throne.

This is the form in which the badge has appeared ever since.

THE FALCON OF THE PLANTAGENETS

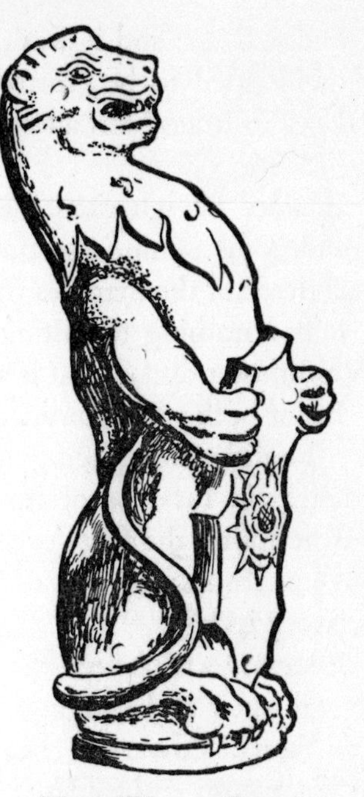

THE WHITE LION OF MORTIMER

IV. *The Black Bull of Clarence*
and
V. *The White Lion of Mortimer*

Both these beasts came to Elizabeth II through Edward IV, and the black bull descended to him by devious paths from Edward III's third son, Lionel, Duke of Clarence, whose beast it must have been, for he had two bulls as supporters on his shield.

At Westminster the black bull's shield was charged with the Royal Arms as borne from 1405 to 1603 by all the sovereigns of Lancaster and Tudor. This shield, France and England quarterly, displayed the leopards of England in the second and third and the French Arms (fleur-de-lis) in the first and fourth quarters.

At Windsor the black bull is included in the Yorkist Beasts erected in 1925 on the roof of St George's Chapel; it may also be seen as one of the King's Beasts at Hampton Court, where it holds a Tudor Rose; and it was one of the Royal Beasts which Elizabeth I caused to be erected on the landing-stage at Greenwich Palace. So it has been a long time in the public eye.

Edward IV inherited the White Lion of Mortimer from his grandmother, Anne Mortimer, heiress of the Mortimers, Earls of March, or of the marches (borders) of Wales.

It had nothing to distinguish it from the Lion of England at Westminster except that it was uncrowned.

But if both were considered in colour it would be noticed that the English Lion, being gold, had a red tongue and claws; whereas in the case of the Lion of Mortimer both were blue. Furthermore, the first (except on a shield) is normally rampant; but sometimes the Lion of Mortimer sits, with tail curled neatly between its legs.

It seems to have been the fashions for royalties of an earlier day to will their bed-hangings, for we read of Edmund Mortimer, grandson of Edward III, bequeathing some of these draperies made of black satin embroidered with white lions and gold roses. The aforesaid Edmund seems to have had a sense of humour, for on one of his seals the lions are shown wearing large helmets topped off with the Mortimers' crest of a plume of feathers.

The shield the Lion of Mortimer bore at Westminster was charged with a white rose encircled by golden rays, known in heraldry as a 'white rose en soleil.' Here again the shield is of the Yorkist livery colours.

This badge is used, with royal permission, by York Herald.

THE BLACK BULL OF CLARENCE

II

Royal Heraldry: The Queen's Beasts

PART TWO

VI. *The Yale of Beaufort*

THE Yale comes to Elizabeth II from Henry VII, the first Tudor King, who inherited it from his mother, Lady Margaret Beaufort.

The yale first appeared in heraldry as a supporter of the shield of arms borne by John, Duke of Bedford, son of Henry IV; but the naturalists of the Middle Ages had described it long before then. Pictures of the yale vary, but the artists all agreed on one point: that this creature could move its horns about as it pleased—and they suggest this characteristic by making one horn point forward and the other backward.

This gives the yale a slightly comic look. One could almost imagine that if it had lived in a world of human beings we might have seen it billed in a variety show as being able to move its ears "in a most unusual and amusing manner."

When the Duke of Bedford died, in 1435, the earldom lapsed; but it was revived a few years later, and bestowed with the dukedom of Somerset on Sir John Beaufort. Hence the adoption of the yale by the Beaufort family, for Sir John took as supporters the eagle and the yale, which had supported the Duke of Bedford's shield. Lady Margaret, his daughter, preferred two yales. Her arms, supported by yales, appear on the gateway of St John's College, Cambridge, which she founded, and also on Christ's College. The Beaufort yale is silver, with spots of gold, and horns, hooves, and tufts of the same colour.

The Yale at Westminster held a shield half white and half blue, the Beaufort colours, on which was a golden portcullis crowned with the arched Royal Crown.

An uncrowned portcullis was a Beaufort badge, and it was also used by Henry VII, both crowned and uncrowned.

It is now used by two of the Heralds—by Somerset Herald crowned and by Portcullis Pursuivant uncrowned, Portcullis being one of the two new Pursuivants instituted by Henry VII on his accession, in 1485.

What would have been the reactions of Lady Margaret Beaufort if she could have looked into the future and seen the golden portcullis as the principal charge on the shield of the Westminster City Council; and the black portcullis which, with two roses, forms the Council's crest, on the city's dustcarts?

Perhaps the fact that the portcullis was introduced both here and in the arms of the Richmond Borough Council as a reminder of close association with the Sovereign might have softened the blow, for Henry VII, who was Earl of Richmond in Yorkshire, renamed his Palace of Sheen Richmond.

VII. *The White Greyhound of Richmond* *and* VIII. *The Red Dragon of Wales*

These two beasts are in a kind of partnership, for they both go back to days long before the battle of Bosworth, in 1485; but as it was again Henry VII with whom they were so particularly associated they may be looked upon as especially *his* beasts.

As Edward III with the falcon, so Henry VII with the greyhound. Sometimes he had two as supporters, at other times a dragon and a greyhound.

(The custom of changing supporters went out in the time of James I.)

On two of Henry VII's standards the greyhound appeared; and in due course (with other Beasts) it surmounted the royal pavilion when Henry VIII spent a small fortune on the Field of the Cloth of Gold in France, in the year 1513.

The white greyhound was the special beast of the honour (estate) and earldom of Richmond, Yorkshire, and was inherited by Henry VII from his father, Edmund Tudor, created Earl of Richmond in 1453.

The shield which the White Greyhound held at Westminster was charged with the Tudor Rose crowned and set in a shield of the Tudor white-and-green livery.

The Red Dragon, which is one of the Queen's Beasts, is of Welsh origin. Henry VII adopted it as a sign that he was descended from Cadwalader, and it was used by all Tudor sovereigns as well as by Henry VII's daughter Margaret, through whom Elizabeth II inherited both the Crown and the Dragon.

It is difficult to think of a period in history when there wasn't a dragon in the world.

In Christian times it stood for the Devil, yet, for all its wickedness, so great was its strength and wisdom that both in West and East emperors and kings adopted it as an emblem.

In the early histories of Wales the dragon is often mentioned. Owen Tudor, Henry VII's grandfather, took it as his device, and it was later used by his sons both as crest and supporter. It has been told of Cadwalader, Owen Tudor's Welsh ancestor, that at a time when his world had almost crashed about his ears he was cheered by hearing that one day a descendant of his would wear the crown of England.

Perhaps this was why one of the standards borne by Henry VII on Bosworth Field and offered afterwards in St Paul's Cathedral was a red dragon on white-and-green silk; and just as he created the new office of Portcullis Pursuivant in honour of his mother's family, so Henry VII instituted Rouge Dragon Pursuivant to commemorate his paternal Welsh origin.

When Great Britain and Ireland were united in 1801 a red dragon walking on a green mount was stated to be the King's badge for Wales; and a hundred years later Edward VII gave the same creature, differenced by a silver label, as a badge to be borne by the Prince of Wales as well as the ostrich feathers.

But when it was represented that the heir to the throne ought to

The Yale of Beaufort

The White Greyhound of Richmond

The Red Dragon of Wales

have not merely a badge of the Principality, from which his chief title derived, but something in his arms, King George V, in 1911, decided that Prince Edward (now the Duke of Windsor), and his successors as Princes of Wales, should set in the middle of the shield a small shield like that held by the Red Dragon at Westminster; and later, in 1953, Elizabeth II ordered that the badge of Wales should from that time on be the Red Dragon, charged on a shield half white and half green. Around the shield is a riband bearing the motto *Y DDRAIGGOCH DDYRY CYCHWYN*—'The red dragon gives the lead.'

The shield held by the Dragon at Westminster was divided into four quarters, two gold and two red, the gold quarters bearing a red leopard, and the red quarters bearing a gold one—in other words, four counter-tinctured lions.

THE UNICORN OF SCOTLAND

THE WHITE HORSE OF HANOVER

These quartered arms are the arms of Wales, and are based very closely on those of Owen Glendower.

IX. *The Unicorn of Scotland*

When Queen Elizabeth I died, in 1603, the English Crown passed to James VI of Scotland, who then became James I of England. He thereupon took as his supporters in England a Lion of England and one of his Scottish unicorns; and the lion and the unicorn have been the supporters of the Royal Arms of the United Kingdom ever since.

How the unicorn came to be taken as a Scottish royal beast is still shrouded in mystery. We can read of Unicorn Pursuivant in 1426, and James III of Scotland struck gold coins which were called unicorns because on one face sat a unicorn supporting a shield of Scotland. It was not, however, until the latter part of the sixteenth century that two unicorns were adopted as the regular supporters of the Royal Arms of Scotland.

Legends flourish about the unicorn. In appearance it is quite one of the most presentable of the mythical bestiary. Head, body, and mane of a horse, slim legs like those of an antelope, and a little tuft of a beard; and of course the long twisted horn which gives the creature its name, and which it took from the narwhal, or sea-unicorn.

Yet in one description of a unicorn (a pre-Christian one) it figures as being so huge that it could not be got into the ark, so it had to be towed behind, and so strong that it could spike an elephant on its horn.

But the Christian unicorn was very different: a small animal, no bigger than a kid, with one sharp horn.

One legend says that the unicorn was a kind of water-taster for the rest of the animal world, and that it had only to stir a stagnant or even poisonous pool of water with its horn to make it pure and sweet.

The Royal Coat-of-arms of Scotland is of gold charged with a red lion ramping in a royal tressure (the double frame decked inside and out with fleurs-de-lis), and this is the coat which King James introduced into the British Royal Arms, and that is the shield which the Unicorn held at Westminster. The Scottish Unicorn is white, with horn, mane, tufts, hooves, collar, and chain all of gold.

X. *The White Horse of Hanover*

The White Horse came into the Royal Arms when Queen Anne died in 1714, for the crown of Britain then passed to the Elector of Hanover, who styled himself George I, King of Great Britain, France, and Ireland, Duke of Brunswick-Lüneburg.

The Royal Arms had been changed in 1707 following the union of the two kingdoms of England and Scotland. Now came another change to include the arms of King George's German dominions. The result is the shield which was held by the White Horse at Westminster: divided into four quarters, in the first are the leopards of England and the Scottish lion set side by side, as was ordained in 1707; in the second and third are the fleur-de-lis of France and the Irish harp respectively; and in the fourth are the arms of Brunswick-Lüneburg (Hanover).

The coat of Hanover is divided into three, as though by an inverted "Y." First, the *two* golden leopards of Brunswick; next, the blue lion of Lüneburg; at the foot, a white horse running on a red field; and in the centre of the whole is a little red shield charged with the golden crown of Charlemagne—symbol of an office held by the Elector of Hanover.

The arms of Brunswick (two golden leopards) are supposed to date back to an English princess, Matilda or Maud, daughter of Henry II. This gives credence to the old legend that Henry bore these arms himself. They were afterwards changed by his son, Richard I, to *three* lions. (Matilda married Henry V (the Lion), Duke of Saxony, ancestor of the House of Guelph.)

But white horses had galloped many thousands of miles round a good many fields since the day, perhaps, when Hengist and Horsa landed on these shores, before the era of heraldry—for both these names mean horse. That was about fifteen hundred years ago.

The White Horse of Hanover always runs, while the White Horse of Kent rears; but that again might be something to do with the shape of the shield and the space that was available.

The White Horse of Kent used to adorn the front of some English steam-rollers. We can see it any day on the uniforms of the Queen's Own Royal West Kent Regiment, and on the caps and blazers of the Kent County Cricket Club, to mention only a few places.

There is an interesting connexion between the arms of Lüneburg and those of Prince Philip, Duke of Edinburgh. The first quarter of Prince Philip's shield bears the Royal Arms of Denmark, which are the source from which Lüneburg derives its blue lion on gold, for in the thirteenth century Duke Otto adopted it in honour of his mother, who was a princess of Denmark. In both cases the golden field is powdered with red hearts.

12

Heralds and their Duties

The Rise of the Experts

FOR the first two centuries of heraldry there was little or no control—the only copyright was one of custom rather than legality.

Yet there must have been some sort of code, for it was not till the year 1300 that a clash occurred, when two knights turned up at the siege of Caerlaverock bearing the same device. The knights, Sir Brian Fitzalan and Sir Hugh Poyntz, caused great surprise to the spectators by doing so; but nobody, apparently, was more surprised than they were themselves.

But when the heraldry business threatened to assume unmanageable proportions the reigning King, Henry V, decreed that in future no gentleman should "bear arms" without permission either from himself or from the Heralds.

Henry knew quite well what he was about when he put the Heralds in charge. First heard of in the British Isles in the reign of Edward I (1272–1307), they already looked after such matters as the arrangements for tournaments, where they kept the score and acted as umpires. And they were learnéd in coat armour—they had to be, for one of their duties was to cry aloud the knight's name as he entered the lists: if his visor was down how could they know the name except by the arms?

Another of the Heralds' duties was to journey to the Continent when a tournament was in prospect to invite entries. (Looked at through twentieth-century eyes, this seems a slow job. The arrangements for tournaments must have been years in the making.)

The Continent reached, the Heralds set about making inquiries, and began to take names. Those who signified their desire to take part in the tournament were guaranteed a safe conduct; and the Heralds returned to England to get on with the preparations.

In due course the competitors began to arrive in this country, wearing surcoats, and fully armed (shields, banners, horse-trappings), with their attendant esquires, who carried pennons and lances.

The Heralds then examined credentials. When each competitor had passed he hung up his shield and crested helm in the place indicated to him, and as soon as preparations were completed the public were allowed to have a look round, to see what they would be getting for their money on the great day: a kind of preview.

Knights were then ready to give or receive challenges for anything in the nature of a private tussle. Knight A, walking round the display of shields, might see something that annoyed him in the achievement of Knight B, C, D, or E, and feel that he would like to engage him in single combat. He would thereupon tap that gentleman's shield with the particular weapon he proposed to use, and a Herald standing by for the purpose (presumably he would be able to write) took down details, and recorded the challenge as something to be fought out during the period of the tournament.

Perhaps it was because of all this work and responsibility that Henry V created the new office of Garter King-of-Arms, as he did about the year 1415; and from then until now there has been a Garter King-of-Arms, whose duty it is among others to proclaim a new sovereign.

The Heralds, generally speaking, attend coronations, Openings of Parliament, Proclamations of the Sovereign's Accession, Services of the Order of the Garter, and Garter King's introduction of new peers into the House of Lords.

Seventy years or so after the appointment of the first Garter King-of-Arms another King, Richard III (Crookback), gave the Heralds their first Charter; and the Heralds' College, or College of Arms, was set up. Now the science of heraldry was really established.

But it must be remembered that even before that date a vast

number of coats-of-arms had been drawn (emblazoned) and described (blazoned) in heraldic language on long narrow strips of parchment which were called Rolls of Arms, and it is from them that a good deal of our knowledge of the old Armory has been acquired, though they were by no means complete.

MEDIEVAL ROLL OF ARMS

In the fifteenth, sixteenth, and seventeenth centuries the Heralds travelled into various parts of England, setting up courts of inquiry in the big towns, to which armigerous persons were invited to bring their coats-of-arms for inspection.

If any irregularities were discovered these were corrected, and if anyone was thought to be unlawfully bearing arms he was required to bring more evidence to prove his case or give up his claim to be a gentleman.

The earliest of these visitations, as they were called, took place in 1413, and they were held at intervals of about thirty years, the last one being in 1686.

It is the men, and not the bricks and mortar, that constitute the College of Arms. They have kept their files and documents in various buildings since the days of Richard III.

The present College of Arms, a beautiful house in Queen Victoria Street, London, one of the City's few remaining historic buildings, is on the site of the building given to the College by Queen Mary in 1555.

On Thursday, May 24, 1956, the American Ambassador to England formally opened the new iron gates, which are the gift of Mr Blevins Davis, an American admirer of this country.

And in the issue of the *Sunday Times* for May 20, 1956, we read:

> If funds permit it is [also] hoped to carry out the long-cherished project of establishing a museum in which the priceless treasures in possession of the College may be on permanent exhibition to the public. The College has the site but very little money.
>
> An exhibition of its treasures held in 1934 astonished every one by the beauty and historic interest of the exhibits. . . .
>
> It is felt by everybody concerned that these possessions, which reflect so much of the history of this country, should no longer be kept hidden from the public eye.

N.B. The 1934 Exhibition, though not the most recent, was on a larger scale than any succeeding it.

The Heralds are very busy men. Here are their names:

Garter Principal King-of-Arms. (In Scotland the corresponding position is filled by *Lord Lyon King-of-Arms.*)
Clarenceux King-of-Arms.
Norroy and Ulster King-of-Arms.

In olden times Clarenceux had to look after all those duties connected with heraldry in the parts of England south, east, and west of the Trent; Norroy north of the Trent. They still do this, but, in addition, Norroy is responsible for Ulster. Garter King-of-Arms looks after Wales.

Next come the six Heralds attached to the College of Arms. They are:

Windsor	*Somerset*
Chester	*York*
Richmond	*Lancaster*

In the third rank come the Pursuivants of Arms, with their picturesque names:

Rouge Croix, Blue Mantle, Rouge Dragon, Portcullis

There is also a special class of Heralds, appointed to carry out ceremonial functions on such occasions as coronations or Garter investitures. They have magnificent titles such as

Maltravers Herald Extraordinary
Norfolk Herald Extraordinary
Fitzalan Pursuivant Extraordinary

The Heralds, on State occasions, wear feathered hats and a wonderful garment called a 'tabard,' which resembles the surcoat of the Middle Ages, and which is embroidered on back, front, and sleeves with the Royal Arms. Though the tabard is the same in style for all the Heralds, the material of which it is made differs according to rank, that of the Kings-of-Arms being of velvet, the Heralds of satin, and the Pursuivants of silk damask. Kings-of-Arms, in addition, have a special coronet, which they wear at coronations, and which is shown in the illustration on page 77.

The Earl Marshal, who is over all the Heralds, is always a Duke of Norfolk, the office being hereditary.

When Richard III gave the Heralds their Charter he created the then Duke of Norfolk Earl Marshal, asking him to take over Westminster Abbey, and prepare it for his Coronation. Held at first intermittently by members of the Howard family, the office became permanent in 1677.

Richard was crowned over four hundred and seventy years ago; but since then coronations of a sovereign have for the most part been organized by the male descendants of that Duke of Norfolk.

Medieval herald

Present-day herald: Garter Principal King-of-Arms

The Heralds have other things to do besides making arrangements for State occasions. Among their varied duties is that of tracing pedigrees and advising those who wish to "take out arms."

When arms have been (*a*) confirmed—for example, in a case where there has been some uncertainty which is now resolved, or (*b*) granted—it is the King-of-Arms alone who can grant arms, under the authority of the Earl Marshal—the grants and confirmations are duly recorded with a full emblazonment of the insignia at the College of Arms.

13

Heraldry in Westminster Abbey

The Ancient Shields in the Nave Aisles

IF you look at a book which has to do with Westminster Abbey you may see on the cover an illustration of this shield. And inside the Abbey you will see the shield itself carved and painted, bearing the so-called arms of Edward the Confessor, at

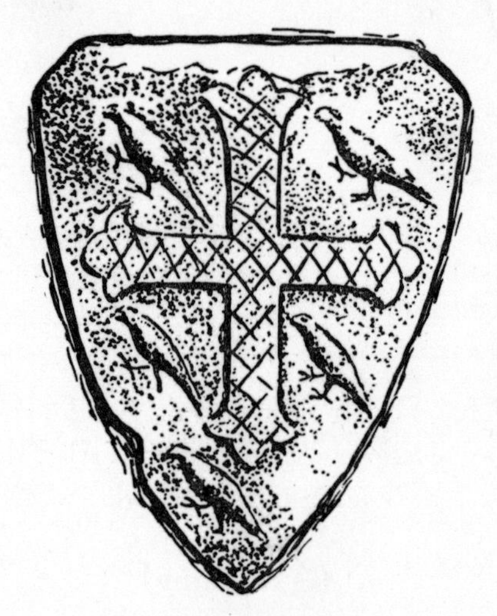

ARMS OF EDWARD
THE CONFESSOR

the east end of the south wall, five doves, and a cross named 'patonce' (splayed ended). Edward the Confessor was buried in Westminster Abbey, at first west of the High Altar, but afterwards in the shrine built to receive him by order of Henry III, in the centre of the Confessor's Chapel, "the most sacred spot in the Abbey."

The colours in this shield, like those in others in the same group, are faded with age now, but originally the cross and doves were of gold on a blue ground.

We have used the phrase "so-called arms of Edward the Confessor" because this monarch lived before the days of heraldry, and these arms were allotted to him after his death.

Yet we can hardly call them faked, for on one of his coins the Confessor showed a cross between four doves; and the arms were based upon that. The fifth dove was added to fill up the space at the foot of the shield.

In course of time the doves turned into 'martlets'—little birds much used in heraldry. (You will remember that a martlet is one of the cadency marks.) They are shown without feet (often without beaks too), for they were identified with swallows; and legend says that swallows never stand upon the ground, so they do not need feet.

It was Henry III who placed the shield—with others—on the walls, for in 1245 he had decided to pull down and rebuild some of the Abbey, enlarging other parts. No one quite knows why he decided to do this. Some say that he had been much impressed with the beauty of Salisbury Cathedral; others that he wanted to make a kind of St Edward the Confessor Shrine as a counter-attraction to the new Becket Shrine at Canterbury; and he may have seen—at any rate he had heard about—the glories of the new cathedrals in northern France, and was suffering from an envy complex.

Encouraged by his artist-monk friend, Matthew Paris, he made use of the decorative uses of heraldry by ordering his craftsmen to place sixteen stone shields, bearing the arms of the subscribers to the building-fund, in the nave aisles.

Of these sixteen shields, some of which were probably carved and painted by Matthew Paris himself, fourteen remain, though some have been moved from their original positions.

Next to the Confessor's arms, Henry III placed his own: *Gules three lions* (leopards) *passant guardant palewise or—i.e.*, a red shield with three gold lions one above the other.

Henry was the third King of England to bear these arms, and they had been in use for seventy years when he placed them on the Abbey wall, and also on the tiled floor of the Chapter House.

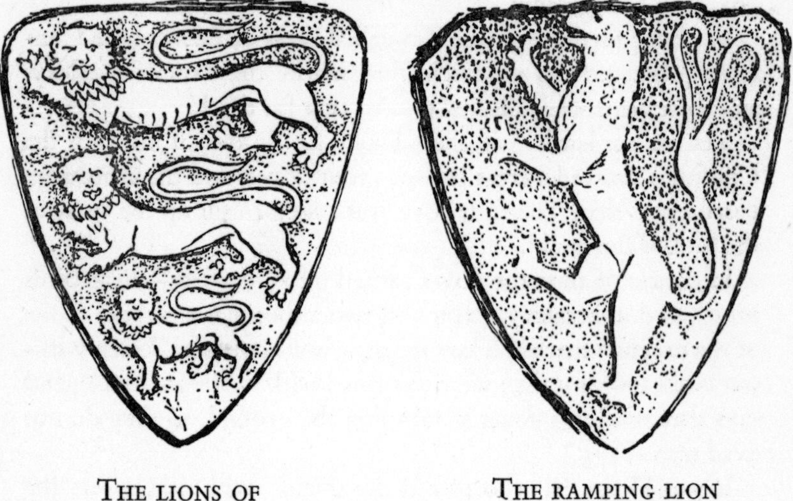

THE LIONS OF ENGLAND

THE RAMPING LION OF DE MONTFORT

One other shield is of very particular interest; it bears the ramping lion of the de Montfort family, with the forked tail raised over its back, and it helps to give a date to the work of rebuilding. In 1264 the mighty Simon de Montfort, brother-in-law and former friend of the King, rose in rebellion against his monarch; so the shield must have been placed before that event, for the King would never have allowed a rebel's shield to be set up in his new church.

The Abbey's Royal Arms

Opposite the entrance to St Edmund's Chapel, on the side of Edward III's tomb, there are four shields enamelled in colours: two bearing the Cross of St George and two showing the first change in the Royal Arms from the three lions.

The King's shield was now quartered: in the first and fourth quarters are the arms sometimes known as 'France Ancient' (fleurs-de-lis), and in the second and third are the lions of England. The fleurs-de-lis were to show that Edward III claimed the throne of France through his mother, Isabel, a French princess.

Edward rather overreached himself by doing this, for he gave a handle to the people who were only too ready to accuse him of mixing politics with heraldry by displaying the arms of a kingdom which he did not possess.

His grandson and successor, Richard II (son of the Black Prince), also bore France Ancient and England quarterly, but combined them with the arms of Edward the Confessor. He is supposed to have done this in order to win favour in Ireland, where St Edward was greatly revered. So Richard, like his grandfather, was not above making use of heraldry for his own ends and purposes.

About 1365 Charles V of France reduced his fleurs-de-lis to the number of three, creating the arms sometimes known as 'France Modern,' or 'New France.'

Henry IV, in the sixth year of his reign, followed suit in the English Royal Arms, which then remained static until the death of Elizabeth I, in 1603 (noted in connexion with the Black Bull's shield at Westminster).

These arms can be seen in many places in the Abbey—to name two of them: on the monument of Henry VII, where the shield is encircled by the Garter, and on the tomb of Elizabeth I.

On the death of Elizabeth I a change came again in the Royal Arms, indicating the accession to the English throne of a Scottish King. The combined arms of France Modern and England remained, but were now placed in the first and fourth quarters of the shield, the Royal Arms of Scotland occupying the second quarter, and the harp of Ireland the third.

These arms remained unchanged until 1688. In the Abbey they are to be seen on the tomb of the baby daughter of King James I, close to Elizabeth I's monument, but they are placed on a lozenge, not a shield. Among women only a reigning queen may place her arms on a shield.

Although there were in fact seven further alterations between the reign of James I and the accession of Queen Victoria, not all the changes in the Royal Arms are represented in the Abbey. The changes can be listed briefly: (*a*) William III and Mary II jointly, in 1689, (*b*) William III alone, in 1694, (*c*) Anne in 1702, (*d*) Anne in 1707, (*e*) George I in 1714, (*f*) George III in 1801, (*g*) George III in 1814, and finally (*h*) Victoria in 1837.

The Royal Arms of King George VI are to be seen in the windows of the Chapter House. Beside them is a second shield in which the Royal Arms are combined with the punning bows and lions of the family of Bowes-Lyon, for his Queen (Queen Elizabeth the Queen Mother).

Two other shields have place in this group, one bearing the arms of the late Queen Mary; and the other, the Royal Arms differenced by a white label with three pendants, on the middle one a rose, and on each of the others a red cross, these being the arms of Queen Elizabeth II when she was Princess Elizabeth.

The Abbey's Royal Badges

Who does not know the 'planta genista,' or broom-plant, the badge first worn by Geoffrey of Anjou, father of Henry II, which gave its name to the Plantagenet line?

In the Abbey sprigs of it are engraved on the robes of the effigy of Richard II, with his personal badges of the white hart and the sun-burst (formerly a badge of Edward III, Richard's grandfather).

There is a fine painting of a white hart on the wall of the Muniment Room; and in the Chapel of Our Lady of the Pew, among the pine-cone pattern on the walls, there is a less imposing little white hart, with a crown round its neck.

Originally also a badge of Edward III's, passed on to his son, the Black Prince (who placed three white feathers on black in his 'shield of peace'), and through him to Richard II, is the ostrich-feather which is introduced into the inscription round Richard's tomb.

From this came the three Prince of Wales's feathers encircled by a coronet, the insignia of the Heir Apparent to the throne, whether he holds the title of Prince of Wales or not.

BADGE OF RICHARD II:
THE WHITE HART

To-day they form the badge of Charles, Prince of Wales.

The cornices of Henry V's chapel are decorated with his badges: antelopes, lighted beacons (cressets), and chained swans. The swan and the antelope came to him from his mother's family, the Bohuns, and the vault above the ambulatory has more Bohun swans and antelopes, couched, and with twisted napkins about their necks.

BADGE OF H.R.H. THE PRINCE OF WALES

BADGES OF HENRY V: ANTELOPE, BEACON, AND CHAINED SWAN

Do you know the lines in Shakespeare's *Henry IV*, where Sir Richard Vernon says:

> I saw young Harry, with his beaver on,
> His cushes on his thighs, gallantly arm'd,
> Rise from the ground like feather'd Mercury,
> And vaulted with such ease into his seat,
> As if an angel dropp'd down from the clouds,
> To turn and wind a fiery Pegasus
> And witch the world with noble horsemanship.

On a beam above his chantry for many years hung Henry's helm and saddle and the shield (probably a ceremonial one). All three were carried at his funeral, and after that ceremony became the property of the Church.

The helm is a genuine tilting one, and once bore a crest; and the saddle, made of wood with a padded seat, is the only one of its kind in existence in England. How one would like to believe that it was the seat into which he "vaulted with such ease."

Roses flower luxuriantly in the Abbey heraldry, and the red-and-white variety are united in the Tudor Rose, to be seen in the decoration of Henry VII's chapel, where there are badges galore—on gates, walls, vaulting, and in the east window.

Three badges in particular we must refer to, though, alas, only two out of the three can be seen; for the first, a hawthorn-tree with a crown above it (commemorating the finding of Richard III's crown under a hawthorn bush at the battle of Bosworth), was in the window which no longer exists (see page 85), behind Henry VII's tomb. It can, however, still be seen on the vaulting of the choir of Winchester Cathedral.

Of the other two, the portcullis inherited from his mother's family, the Beauforts, was crowned by Henry VII when Parliament passed an Act settling the Crown on him and his heirs; and the Tudor Rose (mentioned above) symbolized his marriage with the daughter of Edward IV, the Yorkist King.

The Abbey's Royal Supporters

These, first displayed infrequently by Richard II, make their definite appearance in Royal heraldry in the reign of Henry VI, who used in turn a lion, a panther, and a heraldic antelope. Some kings often had the lion as one supporter, ringing the changes on various animals for the other. The earliest example in the Abbey is seen in the dragon and greyhound of Henry VII, which uphold the Royal Arms over the doors of the bronze screen round his tomb; while pairs of these animals, apparently preparing to attack each other, form part of the decoration of the screen.

BADGES OF HENRY VII:
DRAGON AND GREYHOUND

The dragon kept its place as a Royal Supporter through the Tudor reigns, but a lion supplanted the greyhound, as may be seen on the tomb of Elizabeth I. When James VI of Scotland became James I of England he replaced the Welsh dragon by the Scottish unicorn, and the Lion and the Unicorn have been the Royal Supporters ever since.

The R.A.F. Badges in the Abbey

The Battle of Britain window replaces the most easterly window of Henry VII's chapel, in the Abbey, which was destroyed in the bombing by the enemy during the Second World War.

In it are the heraldic badges of sixty-three Fighter Squadrons of the R.A.F. which took part in the Battle of Britain.

What would the peasant of, say, Edward III's time, who depended on a badge for its brightness and boldness, have felt if he had been able to see that wondrous blaze of colour?

It is a long way to come, from the end of the twelfth century to modern heraldry—nearly eight hundred years. The medieval knight, with his painted shield, wanted to be easily recognizable by his friends; the modern soldier rather seeks to make himself inconspicuous by melting into the background.

But both had the same thought in mind: "safety first."

14

St George's Chapel, Windsor Castle

ANYONE going to Windsor Castle, and bent on heraldry, would probably make a bee-line for the choir in St George's Chapel, where, affixed to the panelling at the back of the stalls, are about seven hundred gilded metal plates, bearing enamelled and painted emblems covering a period of more than five hundred years—from 1421 until the present time.

These 'stall-plates,' as they are called, commemorate the Knights of the Most Noble Order of the Garter, an Order founded by Edward III.

Above the stall of each knight hangs the banner with his coat-of-arms, and on the canopy of his stall is a helmet topped by his crest.

But though on the death of a knight the banner bearing his arms is removed, the stall-plates remain for all time.

The stalls themselves were carved between 1477 and 1483, by which later date the building operations going on in the chapel were sufficiently advanced to allow the choir to be used; and the number of stall-plates now remaining is more than 42 per cent. of the total possible number, the earliest of them having been removed from the first chapel (now the Albert Memorial Chapel) to their present places.

The gaps are accounted for by the fact that some have been stolen, while others were removed when knights disgraced their knighthood. Some were never positioned at all.

The Order of the Garter consists of twenty-five Knight Companions in addition to the Sovereign, sons of the Sovereign, and foreign monarchs.

STALL-PLATE
ST GEORGE'S CHAPEL
WINDSOR CASTLE

Some of the earlier stall-plates commemorate the founder members of the Order, men who fought with the Black Prince. Yet, oddly enough, there are no plates commemorating either the Black Prince himself or his father, Edward III, who founded the Order.

The building operations already referred to spread over a period of years, from 1477 to 1528, for St George's Chapel was built in two stages. The nave was begun when the choir and its aisles were completed, although the stone vaulting was not finished until 1528.

Incidentally, it looks as though the nave might never have been finished at all if it had not been for the munificence of one Sir Reginald Bray, a gentleman in the service of King Henry VII.

This generosity was acknowledged in the number of the memorials to Sir Reginald, who possessed a punning badge: the 'hemp-bray'—an implement for crushing hemp. It is to be met with more than a hundred times in stone, glass, and ironwork throughout the nave, as well as in the Bray Chapel, where the hemp-bray badge is repeated many times along the cornice and even as part of the lock-plate.

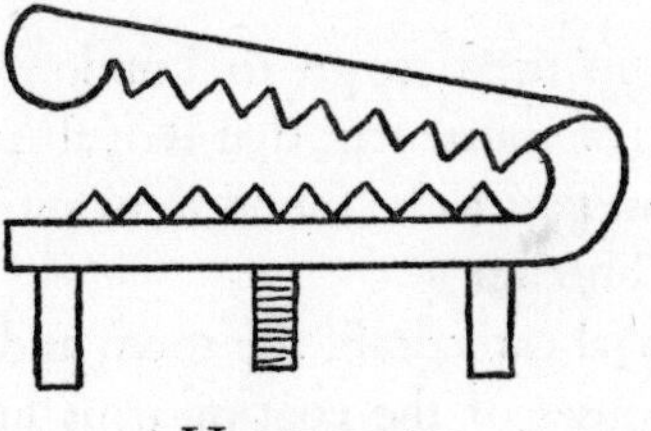

HEMP-BRAY

One wonders if this lavish acknowledgment of his bounty was the way by which the Sovereign (and a mean one at that) made a return for the present of hard cash. Did Sir Reginald strike a bargain with his master, so that the record of his good deeds should go down to posterity?

Though it does not provide the answer to that question, there is a most interesting postscript on the subject to be found in the guide-books, which tell us that Dean Christopher Urswick, *who had been jointly responsible with Sir Reginald Bray for the completion of the nave*, in 1507 established his own memorial chantry in the Urswick Chapel, which had been founded in 1493–94, by two canons and a verger for masses and prayers to be said for their souls. The inscription on the stone base of the screen in front reads:

> O God, who by thy only begotten Son didst redeem mankind, being incarnate of the Virgin's womb and having suffered death, deliver, we beseech Thee, the souls of Henry VII and Christopher, and all those whom Christopher offended during life, from eternal death, and bring them to eternal life. Amen. God have mercy.

Had the two gentlemen quarrelled with each other? Or even with their lord and master, Henry VII?

15

Heraldry in Other Places

THERE is no need to go to London to study heraldry, though it is of course true that Royal Arms and Badges are for the most part to be found in or on London cathedrals, the Abbey, and churches.

But the provincial cathedrals, the town and country churches, are all treasure-houses of the coat-of-arms in stone and stained glass, of the crusader's tomb, the lozenge with the arms of the unmarried lady or widow, the monumental brass plate, in all of which we can read what some one has called "the shorthand of history."

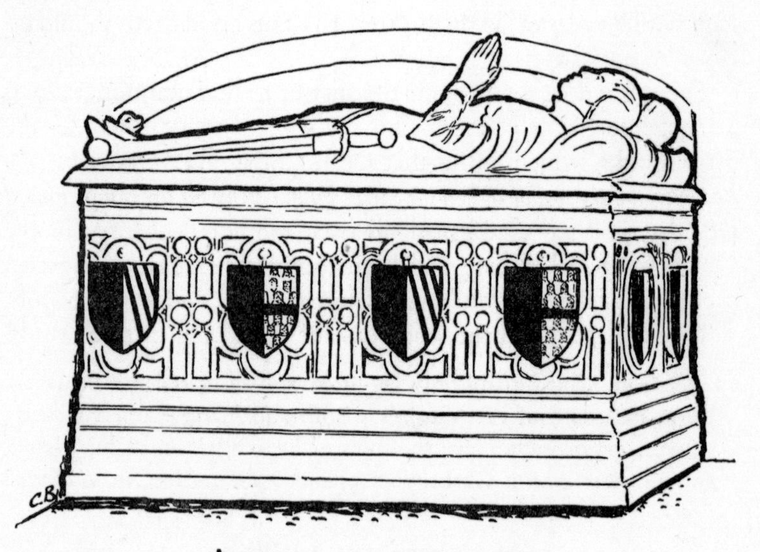

ARMS ON A MEDIEVAL TOMB
STANTON HARCOURT, OXON

"BADGES IN THE CHALK"
FOVANT, WILTS.

Stonework and glass, wood and boiled leather, velvet and silk, have all served as media for the display of heraldic emblems. But can you imagine badges in the chalk? Yet these do exist—under the open sky, on the Wiltshire Downs.

They can be seen by travellers on the main road from London to Exeter near the little village of Fovant (ten miles west of Salisbury): a fine array of enormous regimental badges *carved out in the face of the chalk*. (One of the original badges was a hundred and fifty feet from top to toe.)

The idea of cutting their badge in this unusual medium originated with the London Rifle Brigade, stationed at Fovant in 1916, during the First World War; and though it meant working in off-duty hours (often at crack of dawn to avoid the firing parties on the rifle ranges), volunteers were not lacking for what proved to be a rewarding, though an extremely arduous, job.

Other units followed the example of the London Rifle Brigade, and by the end of the war the hillside recorded pretty accurately the names of the units which had been stationed in the district.

After the departure of the troops there was an interim period, between the two wars, when the growth of weeds and turf, the grazing of sheep and cattle on the hillside, blurred the designs—though some of the regiments paid local workers to keep their own badges in condition.

Fortunately, now, through the efforts and personal donations of generous and interested persons, some of the necessary restoration funds have been got together; and it is hoped that the means will not be lacking to maintain the "Badges in the Chalk"—this unique collection of emblems of national importance, which is attracting visitors from all parts of our own country and from overseas.

16

Heraldry To-day

HERALDRY goes on. The College of Arms grants armorial bearings to newly created peers and others "honoured by the Sovereign," and to corporate bodies (if they have perpetual succession and a common seal).

Even those who cling to the idea that heraldry is just a kind of far-away, dusty history would have to admit that there is one particular section of it, the Royal Arms, which is very much in evidence.

Walking along a suburban street, we see milk being delivered from a trolley emblazoned with the Royal Arms; we glance casually from the window of a bus and notice that a firm of sanitary engineers has been given the right to display the same; a walk through the shopping-quarters of London's West End will provide us with plenty of examples of business houses lucky enough to be "By Appointment to . . ."

In fact, this bit of national heraldry is so familiar to us that we scarcely give it a glance.

Yet a visitor from Texas to this country would quite rightly come to the conclusion that as a nation we are fond of heraldry. If he is here, as he may well be, for a great Royal occasion such as a coronation he will be able to look on at the unfolding of a colourful pageantry which covers hundreds of years.

Moreover, if he stays long enough, and if he is observant, he will discover that the newspapers, normally jealous of every half inch of their space, will yet spare some of it for material pertaining to heraldry: the arms assumed by a newly created peer, an illustration of the Olympic stamps, a reference to the giraffes of Tanganyika, when that territory was visited by an English princess; or information linking ancient with modern, such as occurred when a facsimile of the coat-of-arms of the Cabot family was presented to Sir Miles Thomas, then Chairman of the B.O.A.C., by Philip Cabot, a descendant of the famous John. The coat is displayed in the B.O.A.C. Strato-cruiser *Cabot*, which flies regularly in service on the North Atlantic route.

ARMS OF OXFORD UNIVERSITY

It is the mixture of things that fascinates the visitor from Texas. He has been to Oxford and seen the colleges; some one blazoned for him the arms of the University: *azure a book proper leathered gules, garnished or, having on its dexter side seven seals, the words DOMINUS ILLUMINATIO MEA, between three open crowns proper.*

And those arms date from the middle of the fifteenth century—roughly about a hundred and seventy years before the sailing of the *Mayflower.*

And the day after he came back from Oxford, when he went into a London bank he saw the bank's arms, and of course he asked about them: *argent an eagle displayed sable charged on the body and on each wing with a ducal coronet of the field.* And when he asked the date it was October 22, 1937—hundreds of years in between the two grants of arms. What a difference!

This problematical visitor may well be one of those young Americans who lived in our country during the War. He hadn't time to look into his beginnings then, but he used to wonder if his

English ancestor (an old-time settler) had come from one of those quaint little places dotted about the countryside over here.

However, this time he is going to make more inquiries. He has promised Mom. He had tried to find out something from records before leaving home, but all they seemed to give was a settler's name and perhaps the port he had sailed from, but nothing about his birthplace or home-town. But he has found out that if he is descended from a family which bears arms in this country he has equal rights with the English descendants of that family to bear those arms.

"Yeah! The College of Arms—that's the place for me. But it kinda looks as if it's gonna cost a heck of a lot o' money."

And the young man from Texas is probably right.

ARMS OF
BARCLAYS BANK, LTD

17

The Designing of Arms

THE shield and helm of ancient days still remain the foundation of armorial displays; and to-day, for a good percentage of these, the bookplate is the medium. Were you thinking of a bookplate?

If so, and you are armigerous, go straight ahead. There will be no difficulties. But if not, whose arms were you thinking of displaying?

If you borrow some one else's that may give rise to the idea that the book is also borrowed; and that might prove to be awkward.

The alternative would be to design a non-heraldic bookplate, using a square or oblong instead of a shield (incidentally, much easier); or a round, suggesting a seal. You would then have plenty of choice for your subject: the sea, your own garden, the countryside, the animal world—there is no end to the things from which you might select.

If, purely for your own interest, you mean to study and reproduce, say, some famous shields with the aid of scissors and paste, drawing- and tracing-paper, you will have quite a good time doing it, finding at the end that you have added enormously to your knowledge of heraldry.

Designing arms, however, even if you copy and measure the shields, is not as easy as it looks. Although the old shields, to the casual eye, look as if a child could easily draw them, actually they were designed by 'paynters' of great experience, whose shields were never over-full, and were always well balanced.

You will need to study the proportions of the shield, and on pages 18–21 you will find a set of shields in which are illustrated the proportions of the ordinaries and sub-ordinaries, with reference to the area of the field. This can be varied when used in company with other charges, for a little wangling (sometimes called cheating) is permissible now and then in heraldry. You will find this to be the case when you come to deal with the crest; for though actually the crest should face the same way as the helm which bears it, this arrangement sometimes results in unnatural positions.

An illustration of this wangling is seen in the Royal Arms, where the Lion of England, though guardant, is placed *sideways* across the Royal Helm. This gives a better view of him.

A question which may worry the beginner-artist is: What are the ordinary relative proportions which helm and crest should bear to the shield? And the answer is that a suitable height is three-quarters of the length of the shield: making the helmet too small in proportion to the shield seems to be a trap into which one can fall.

Form in heraldry, as you know, is clear and bold: colours, or tinctures, are few and bright.

When you paint a coat-of-arms you will realize the point of the colour rule: *metal on tincture, tincture on metal.*

Think for a moment of gold and silver (golding and silvering); though a perfect background for colours, on each other you would hardly be able to tell them apart, for they reflect light in the same way. (Incidentally, Chinese white can be used for argent.)

Even yellow (gold) on white would not show up at a distance; and clearness and distinctness are essentials in heraldry. It is for this reason that the birds and beasts are portrayed in a somewhat over-emphasized style: eyes that stare and feet that seem to be almost splayed. This is done to achieve the slight exaggeration that heraldry requires.

Look at your work from time to time through an artist's reducing glass. If you cannot get hold of one try the bottom of a thick tumbler as a substitute.

Postscript

It is probably true that many more people would take up the study of heraldry if it were not for the wording of the blazon of quite simple arms.

The visual side makes a strong appeal; but how are the rather frightening terms, and—still more—the rules of blazon to be absorbed without a good deal of trouble?

It is authoritatively stated that there was a time when heraldic language was much easier to follow, but that the Elizabethan heralds, knowing little and caring less about the subject, covered up their ignorance by using an elaborate system of foreign terms, which have remained in fashion ever since, with others added.

So the question comes up: would not everyday language serve the purpose equally well? And if the study of heraldry is to become really popular isn't the switch-over about due?

Putting under review a few very elementary examples: Why say 'addorsed' when 'back to back' would do instead? Or 'sejant' instead of 'sitting'? And 'salient' instead of 'leaping'?

And surely some words could be got rid of altogether? In early days a 'lozenge' (diamond-shaped figure) was often confused with a 'mascle,' or voided lozenge. But if both were known as lozenges then the word mascle could be wiped out.

And if a girl has golden hair why not say so instead of describing it as 'crined or'?

Stripped of its verbiage, heraldry would no doubt become an easier subject to pursue, yet every subject worth studying has its own special technical terms, seemingly dry-as-dust to the layman but holding no difficulties for the expert. So why not heraldry?

Then let us keep the romantic touch. Let it be gules, argent, azure, not just red, white, blue, though it may take longer.

Speed is not everything. If it were, Queen Elizabeth II would drive on State occasions in the fastest car on the market, instead of in her coach or carriage drawn by Windsor greys and escorted by a detachment of Household Cavalry; and London life would be the poorer, for a flash-back to the fairy-tale world would have disappeared from this all too mechanical age.

Glossary of Heraldic Terms and Expressions

Accessories, paraphernalia belonging to a shield: helmet, wreath (torse), crest, mantling, supporters, motto.
Achievement, the shield and its accessories; a fully marshalled coat.
Addorsed, placed back to back.
Affrontée, full-faced.
Annulet, a ring; the cadency mark of the fifth son.
Antelope, the heraldic one is an imaginary monster sometimes depicted rampant. Probably the "herald paynter's" idea of what an antelope was like.
Appaumée, a hand showing the palm with fingers and thumb erect.
Argent, silver or white.
Armigerous, having a right to arms.
Armorial, pertaining to (heraldic) arms.
Armorial bearings (arms), the hereditary devices painted on a shield, and the accompaniments of a shield.
Armory, sometimes used as an alternative term for heraldry, though strictly speaking it applies to arms alone. (*Archaic*)
Astral Crown (*see* **Crowns and coronets**).
Azure, the heraldic term for blue.
Badge, a distinctive symbol, marking possessions, or worn by retainers: not part of the achievement.
Banner, an oblong or square flag, displaying a man's arms.
Banneret, a knight who, for a brave deed, usually on the field of battle, was entitled to bear a banner instead of a pennon.
Bar, a diminutive of the fesse, occupying one-fifth of the field (of the shield). Some modern heralds regard it as one of the ordinaries.
Baron, the lowest rank in the British peerage.
Baronet, a hereditary knight. (A baronet uses a knight's affrontée helm.)

Barry (barruly), descriptive of the field when divided by horizontal lines into an even number of bars.

Base, the lower part of the shield.

Beacon (cresset), a contrivance to arouse the countryside when an enemy is approaching. It is shown in heraldry as a basket containing fire, on the top of a pillar, against which a ladder is raised.

Bear, to display a shield.

Bearing, a charge or heraldic device.

Bend (*see* **Honourable ordinaries**).

(In) bend, charges placed in a diagonal line as if they were on an invisible bend. (**Bend-wise** is an alternative term.)

Bendlet, a diminutive of the bend; one half its width.

Blazon, the correct description of armorial bearings.

Bordure (*see* **Subordinaries**).

(**à**) **Bouche,** of a shield with the notch in the dexter (right) side, through which the lance was passed when the shield was displayed on the breast.

Bouget (*see* **Water-bouget**).

Brush, a fox's tail.

Bugle, generally blazoned as garnished—*i.e.*, having ribbons round the horn.

Cadency marks, the distinguishing devices which difference the coats-of-arms of the sons in a family, each having his own special mark.

Caduceus, a slender staff, entwined by two serpents, the heads meeting at the top and the tails at the base.

Canting (punning), applied to arms which have any canting (punning) reference to the name of the bearer.

Canton (*see* **Subordinaries**).

Canton sinister, a canton on the sinister side of the shield.

Cap of dignity (*see* **Chapeau**).

Cap of maintenance (*see* **Chapeau**).

Centaur, an imaginary creature, half man and half horse.

Chained, having a chain attached to a collar, the loose end with a ring attached.

Chapeau, the name given by the French to the cap of dignity, or maintenance. It is made of coloured velvet, and turned up with ermine. Originally belonging only to nobles, it is now worn irrespective of rank.

Charge, any simple heraldic figure borne on a shield.

Charged, of the field or ordinaries bearing a device.

Chevron (*see* **Honourable ordinaries**).

Chief (*see* **Honourable ordinaries**).

(In) chief, a charge placed on an imaginary chief or in the upper part of the shield.

Chivalry, the system of knighthood.

Cipher, a monogram of initial letters intertwined together.

Close, of a bird of prey whose wings are folded close to the body.

Closed, of a helmet when the visor is down.

Coat-of-arms (Coat armour), a complete heraldic composition. The term is derived from the old custom of embroidering the armorial bearings of a knight upon his surcoat.

Collared, wearing a collar round the neck.

Collared and chained, wearing round the neck a collar to which a chain is attached.

College of Arms, the Heralds' College, in Victoria Street, London; established somewhere about 1484, when Richard III gave the Heralds their first Charter.

Colours, the heraldic colours may be said to number five—blue, red, black, green, and purple—blazoned respectively as azure, gules, sable, vert, and purpure.

Colour rule, requiring that metal shall not be placed upon metal, nor colour upon colour.

Compartment, the mound or base upon which stand the supporters.

Conjoined, joined together, but not intertwined.

Coronet (*see* **Crowns and coronets**).

Coronet of the Prince of Wales (*see* **Crowns and coronets**).

Couchant (couchée), lying down, but with head raised; applied to animals.

Counter-tinctured (counter-changed), of a field divided per an ordinary or quarterly, in which the charges in each section are of the colour or metal of the opposite section.

Couped, a term used when a head or limb is cut off cleanly from the trunk. An ordinary couped is one that does not reach the edge of the shield.

Crescent, a half-moon with tips uppermost; used as a cadency mark for a second son.

Cresset (*see* **Beacon**).

Crest, part of an achievement of arms, a heraldic device worn on top of a helmet, and next in importance to the shield.

Crined, having hair or a mane.

Cross (*see* **Honourable ordinaries**).

Crosses:

Cross couped, a cross whose arms do not reach the edge of the field.

Cross (of) Calvary, applied to the Passion Cross when mounted on steps heraldically called "grieces."

Cross crosslet, a small cross, with its arms themselves crossed.

Cross engrailed, a cross with the ornamental spikes turned outward.

Cross moline, a cross in which each arm terminates in the form of a millrind—*i.e.*, the iron which is fixed in the centre of a millstone.

Cross quarterly pierced, a cross with the central part cut out, or voided.

Cross patée, a cross of which the limbs, narrow at the centre, expand towards the extremities.

Cross patonce, a cross with splayed ends.

Cross potent, in this cross the four limbs terminate in crutch-like figures (potents).

Crowns and coronets:

Astral Crown, awarded to distinguished members of the Air Force. It is a circle on which are mounted four stars, each star being placed between a pair of elevated wings.

Mural Crown, a circle, masoned and embattled, borne sometimes as a charge, but more often as a crest. It often occurs in arms granted to officers who have distinguished themselves in sieges.

Naval Crown, composed of the sterns and sails of ships arranged alternately on a circle.

Royal Crown, worn only by sovereigns, differing from a coronet in that it has bars arched over the top.

Coronet, in reality a small crown, worn by nobility other than sovereigns.

Coronet of the Prince of Wales, like the Royal Crown, but with one arched bar instead of two.

Mitre, an archbishop's, or bishop's, tall cap, cleft at the top.

Device, a heraldic representation.

Dexter, the right-hand side of the shield, as opposed to sinister (left); as it faces the observer it is actually the left, as the holder would be behind it.

Dexter base (*see* **Points of the shield**).

Dexter chief (*see* **Points of the shield**).

Differences, distinguishing marks inserted into coats-of-arms for the purpose of identifying different persons who bear the same arms.

Differencing, a way of distinguishing the arms of junior members of a family from those of the head.

Dimidiation, the earliest way of marshalling two coats-of-arms on one shield. It was done by dividing the two shields perpendicularly, and adding the dexter half of one to the sinister half of the other.

Displayed (expanded), a term used in speaking of the wings of any kind of bird of prey, but chiefly of an eagle.

Displayed and inverted, when the tips of the open wings are downward, as if the bird intended to alight or take off.

Dragon, an heraldic monster, rather like a crocodile, but with claws and wings, and breath of fire.

Duke, the highest rank in the British peerage.

Eagle, the king of birds, ranking highest among those used in heraldry. The eagle is generally borne displayed.

Earl, the third degree of the British peerage.

Earl Marshal, the head of the College of Arms. This office is held by the Duke of Norfolk, in whose family it is hereditary.

Elevated, applied to wings spread out with tips upward.

Embattled (*see* **Ornamental lines**).

Emblazon, to depict arms in their actual tinctures.

Emblazoning, depicting arms in their actual tinctures.

Engrailed (*see* **Ornamental lines**).

Ensign, a banner or flag.

Ermine, the commonest fur in heraldry, white with black spots.

Escallop (*see* **Shell**).

Escutcheon (scutcheon), an heraldic shield.

Escutcheon of pretence, a smaller shield placed in the chief point of a husband's shield, to signify that his wife is an heraldic heiress.

Esquire, legally a commissioned officer of the Sovereign, the eldest son of a younger son of a peer (and his sons in perpetual succession); the eldest son of a viscount, baron, baronet, or knight; now used indiscriminately as a form of address.

Estoile, a star of six wavy points, unless otherwise described.

Expanded (*see* **Displayed**).

Falcon, a bird which resembles the eagle, except that its head and neck are not tufted but smooth.

Falcon and fetterlock, the well-known badge of John of Gaunt; really a combination of two badges.

Fesse point (*see* **Points of the shield**).

Fetterlock, a shackle or padlock strongly resembling a handcuff.

Field, the whole surface of the shield. In a blazon the tincture of the field is always named first.

File (*see* **Label**).

Flanches (*see* **Subordinaries**).

Fleur-de-lis, the conventional form of the lily. The heraldic kind differs from that of the garden by having three petals instead of five.

Floretée, with fleur-de-lis issuing from ends or sides (*i.e.*, a cross floretée).

France ancient, the royal arms of France bearing many fleurs-de-lis.

France modern, the royal arms of France bearing three fleurs-de-lis.

Fret (*see* **Subordinaries**).

Fusil (*see* **Subordinaries**).

Garb, a sheaf of grain (unless otherwise stated, of wheat).

Garnished, decorated; the term is used to express the ornament set on any charge.

Garter, a circular buckled strap or riband, usually bearing an order of knighthood.

Grand-quarter, a quarter which is subdivided into other quarterings.

Griffin (gryphon), an imaginary animal, the upper half that of an eagle with ears, the lower that of a lion.

Gules, the heraldic term for the colour red.

Gyron (giron) (*see* **Subordinaries**).

Gyronny, divided into a number of gyrons.

Hatching, the system of dots and lines introduced by the seventeenth-century engravers to indicate colours on their black-and-white illustrations.

Hatchment, the armorial bearings of a deceased person displayed on a square or lozenge; formerly placed on the front of a house, but now only seen in churches.

Heater-shaped, a shield shaped like a flat-iron.

Heiress, a heraldic heiress is one who, when her father dies (he being armigerous), has no brothers, and so inherits her father's arms, with the right to transmit them to her children, if she has any.

Helm (*see* **Helmet**).

Helmet (Helm), an iron cap to protect the head and neck. In heraldry the helmet, or helm, displays the crest, and is usually placed above the shield of arms.

Hemp-bray (hemp-brake), an instrument formerly used to break or bruise hemp.

Heralds, the officers whose duty it is to marshall processions, superintend ceremonies. They are (1) **Garter Principal King-of-Arms, Clarenceux King-of-Arms**, and **Norroy and Ulster King-of-Arms**; (2) the six Heralds attached to the College of Arms: **Chester, Lancaster, Richmond, Somerset, Windsor, York**; (3) the Pursuivants: **Blue Mantle, Portcullis, Rouge Dragon, Rouge Croix.** Over them all is the Duke of Norfolk, Earl Marshal of England.

Herald Extraordinary, one of a special class of Heralds, appointed to carry out ceremonial functions on such occasions as coronations or investitures.

Heraldic, pertaining to heraldry.

Heraldry, the science which deals with the proper descriptions of armorial bearings (arms).

Honour point (*see* **Points of the shield**).

Honourable ordinaries (ordinaries), the nine principal ordinaries. These are as follows:

Chief, the upper part of the shield.

Fesse, a broad horizontal band across the middle of the field.

Pale, a broad vertical band down the middle of the field.

Bend, a broad diagonal band from the dexter chief to the sinister base.

Bend sinister, a broad diagonal band from the sinister chief to the dexter base.

Chevron, a figure shaped like an inverted "V," with the lower ends of the 'arms' placed on the dexter and sinister base points.

Pile, the shape of a wedge issuing from the chief, and tapering to a point in the middle base of the shield.

Cross, a vertical and a horizontal band intersecting.

Saltire, the figure known as St Andrew's Cross—*i.e.*, a combination of a bend and a bend sinister.

Honour point, that part of the shield next above the centre.

Hoofed, having hoofs of a different tincture from the rest of the body.

Impalement (impaling), the arranging of two coats-of-arms side by side in one shield.

Indented (*see* **Ornamental lines**).

Inescutcheon, a small shield borne as a charge on another; not to be confused with an escutcheon of pretence.

Invected (*see* **Ornamental lines**).

Inescutcheon of pretence (*see* **Escutcheon of pretence**).

Inflamed, with fire issuing therefrom.

Jagged, applied to the divisionary lines of a field or the outlines of an ordinary, when they are irregular as if the two edges had been torn asunder violently.

Kings-of-Arms (*see* **Heralds**).

Kite-shaped, of one of the earliest forms of shield used in heraldry, slightly convex, long, and pointed.

Knight, one on whom the order of knighthood has been conferred. In feudal times the term was applied to a man on reaching a certain military rank.

Knight Banneret (*see* **Banneret**).

Label (file), a narrow bar in chief with three (or five) pendants; the mark of cadency for an eldest son.

Lancaster, Red Rose of, the badge of the House of Lancaster.

Leek, the badge of Wales.

Leopard, the archaic description of a lion passant guardant; the lions of England at one time were so blazoned.

Lion, the most popular and most frequently used charge in heraldry.

Lists, enclosed places for holding tournaments.

Livery, clothing of distinctive colouring issued by a lord to his followers.

Livery colours, the colours adopted by families for the use of their servants.

Livery companies, London City companies which at one time had distinctive costumes.

Lozenge (*see* **Subordinaries**).

Mantling (lambrequin), ornamental accessory hanging from the back of the helmet wreath. Unless otherwise stated it is of the first mentioned colour in the blazon, and lined with the first metal. Originally used to protect the Crusaders' helmets from the hot sun in Palestine. (The royal mantling is of gold lined with ermine.)

Marquess, the second rank in the British peerage. (It should never be spelt Marquis.)

Marshal of England (*see* **Earl Marshal**).

Marshalling, arranging charges on a shield.

Martlet, the heraldic swallow, always drawn without feet; the cadency mark of the fourth son.

Masoned, said of a castle, when the divisional lines of the cement are represented, thus creating the effect of a wall or stone building.

Middle base (*see* **Points of the shield**).

Middle chief (*see* **Points of the shield**).

Mitre (*see* **Crowns and coronets**).

Moline (*see* **Crosses**).

Motto, a word, phrase, or sentence adopted at will, and borne on a scroll under the coat armour, and sometimes above the crest.

Mullet, the rowel of a spur with five straight points; if it has more it is considered to be a star. The cadency mark of the third son.

Mural Crown (*see* **Crowns and coronets**).

Murrey, a reddish purple; rarely used in heraldry.

Naval Crown (*see* **Crowns and coronets**).

Narwhal, sea-unicorn.

Nebuly (nebulée) (*see* **Ornamental lines**).

Or, the metal gold.

Orle (*see* **Subordinaries**).

Ornamental lines, dividing, or partition, lines used in a combination of two of the tinctures on a shield; also shown in a more ornamental form, such as:

- **Engrailed,** composed of semi-circular notches, with the points outward.
- **Invected,** the opposite of engrailed—*i.e.*, with the points inward.
- **Indented,** notched like a saw.
- **Embattled (imbattled),** shaped like the battlements of a tower.
- **Wavy,** wave-like, as a rule represented by three curves.
- **Nebuly (nebulée),** an exaggerated form of wavy.
- **Raguly (ragulée),** with serratée projections.

Pale (*see* **Honourable ordinaries**).

Palewise, set in the form or direction of a pale.

Pall (*see* **Subordinaries**).

Panther, blazoned by heralds as having fire issuing from its mouth and ears; position generally guardant.

Passant, of an animal walking with one foot raised, and the head in profile.

Passant guardant, of an animal walking with the head affrontée.

Patonce (*see* **Crosses**).

Pearls, the name given to the silver balls seen on some peers' coronets.

Peer, the title given to every nobleman of Great Britain. There are five degrees to the peerage: duke, marquess, earl, viscount, and baron.

Pegasus (*plural*, **pegasi**), the winged horse, a fanciful heraldic beast.

Pellet, a black roundel.

Pendant (pendent), dropping or hanging.

Pennon, a small flag with one or two points. It is pronounced pennant.

Penoncel (pensil), a small pennon.

Per, by means of.

Pile (*see* **Honourable ordinaries**).

Planta genista, the broom plant: the famous badge of the Plantagenet family.

Points of the shield, the important parts of a shield.

They are, from the point of view of the person who is holding the shield, as follows:

Dexter chief, the right-hand side of the chief.

Middle chief, the upper central part of the shield (better known as the "centre chief").

Sinister chief, the left-hand side of the chief.

Fesse-point, the centre of the shield.

Middle base, also known as the "centre base"; that part of the shield close to the lower point.

Dexter base, the right-hand side of the base of the shield.

Sinister base, the left-hand side of the base of the shield.

Honour point, that part of the shield next above the centre.

Portcullis, an instrument for defending a gateway, before which it hung by chains; similar to a grating, with the vertical bars spiked.

Potent, an heraldic fur; also a crutch.

Powdered (Poudrée), said of charges scattered over the field.

Punning (*see* **Canting**).

Purpure, the heraldic term for purple.

Pursuivant (*see* **Heralds**).

Quartering, having several coats marshalled on one shield.

Quarterly, of a shield divided into four equal sections by vertical and horizontal lines. When divided into more than four the blazon must specify quarterly of six, of eight, etc.

Quarterly quartered, a term used when a quartered shield has one or more of its quarters quartered.

Ragged staff, part of the famous badge (Bear and the Ragged Staff) of Warwick, the Kingmaker. The staff is notched.

Raguly (ragulée) (*see* **Ornamental lines**).

Rampant, of an animal standing erect on one hind-leg, the other three raised.

Rampant guardant, as rampant, but with head looking towards the spectator.

Rampant reguardant, as rampant guardant, but looking back.

Red hand, a sinister hand, erect and open, and couped at the wrist. It is the distinguishing badge of baronets, other than those of Nova Scotia creation.

Roundel, a round charge, flat when of metal, and spherical when of colour.

Sable, the heraldic term for black.

Saltire (*see* **Honourable ordinaries**).

Scallop (*see* **Shell**).

Scroll, one of the ornaments of a shield, whereon the motto is written.

Sejant, in a sitting posture.

Serrated, notched like a saw.

Shamrock, the badge of Ireland.

Shell (scallop, escallop), the badge of pilgrims visiting a holy shrine.

Shield, the escutcheon, in blazonry known as the field, the most important part of an armorial composition.

Sinister, the left-hand side of the shield, as opposed to dexter (right); as it faces the observer it is actually the right.

Sinister base (*see* **Points of the shield**).

Sinister chief (*see* **Points of the shield**).

Spur rowel (*see* **Mullet**).

Stall-plate, a plate of gilt-copper upon which the arms of a Knight of the Garter or the Bath are emblazoned.

Standard, an oblong flag narrowing towards the point, originally allowed to none of a lower degree than a knight banneret. The Royal Standard is now rectangular.

Statant, standing; applied to an animal having its four feet on the ground and looking before it, with head in profile.

Steeled, in heraldry this means tipped, or headed, when speaking of weapons.

Subordinaries, a group of devices, less simple, but next in importance to the honourable ordinaries. They are:

- **Bordure (border),** a border to the edge of the shield, supposed to occupy one-fifth of its surface.
- **Inescutcheon,** a small shield borne within the shield as a charge.
- **Orle,** the narrow border of a shield, charged upon the field of a larger shield but detached from the edge.
- **Tressure,** a diminutive of the orle, supposed to be one-half of the width of a charge.

Canton, a square, somewhat less than a quarter of the shield, which is placed in the dexter chief.

Gyron, formed by two straight lines, one issuing from the dexter chief, and one from the dexter fesse, meeting at an acute angle at the fesse-point.

Flanches, borne in pairs; formed by segments of a circle, and placed on the sides of the shield.

Lozenge, a diamond-shaped figure, used instead of a shield for the emblazoning of a lady's arms.

Fusil, similar to a lozenge, but more elongated.

Billet, a small, oblong, rectangular figure, placed standing on one of its shorter sides.

Mascle, a lozenge, voided or perforated.

Fret, a figure formed by the intertwining of a mascle and a narrow saltire.

Roundels (roundles), circular forms, specially indicated according to their tinctures—*e.g.*, roundel or, bezant; roundel argent, plate.

Pall, a charge in the form of the letter "Y": the upper part of a saltire conjoined to the lower part of a pale.

Label, a piece of silk or linen with (generally) three pendants.

Sunburst, rays of the sun emerging from behind a cloud.

Supporters, figures placed on either side of a shield, as if supporting it; part of the achievement of the Royal Family, the higher grades of knighthood, such as Knights Grand Cross, and a few others to whom special permission has been given to display supporters; also of corporate bodies.

Surcoat, a loose sleeveless coat worn by fighting men over their armour.

Tabard, the name given to the surcoat richly embroidered with the Sovereign's Arms, and worn by the Heralds on ceremonial occasions; used by nobility in the early days of heraldry.

Thistle, the badge of Scotland.

Thunderbolt, a twisted bar in pale, in heraldry, inflamed at each end, surmounting two jagged darts in saltire, between two wings expanded, with fire issuing from the centre.

Tincture, the heraldic colour.

Torse (*see* **Wreath**).

Tournament, the medieval military sport.

Trapper, a horse-covering.

Tressure (*see* **Subordinaries**).

Uncharged, plain; bearing no device.

Unicorn, a fabulous beast resembling a small horse, but having a twisted horn projecting from its forehead, a lion's tail, and antelope's feet. Gold coin struck by James III of Scotland.

Vair, one of the heraldic furs.

Vert, the heraldic term for green.

Viscount, the fourth rank in the British peerage. Originally an earl's deputy, the title was made a hereditary degree of honour by Henry VI in 1429.

Visitations, the courts of inquiry into the authenticity of arms, conducted by the heralds in big towns during the fifteenth, sixteenth, and seventeenth centuries. The last one was held in 1686.

Visor, the part of the helmet which protects the face: it can be opened or shut at will.

Voided, perforated or pierced.

Volant, flying.

Wavy (*see* **Ornamental lines**).

Water-bouget, a vessel to hold water.

Winged, having wings.

Wreath (torse), the twisted silk roll which surrounds the helm, hiding the joints between the crest and the top of the helm, keeping the mantling (lambrequin) in place.

Wyvern, a fabulous monster like the dragon, but with only two feet.

Yale, a fabulous beast rather like an antelope, but with the fangs of a lion. Its great feature is that it has two horns which rotate independently, and they are generally represented one pointing forward and the other backward.

York, White Rose of, the badge of the House of York.

An Additional List of some Heraldic Terms which should prove useful to any student of Heraldry

Abased, applied to an ordinary when placed below its usual position.

Accosted, side by side.

Aislée, winged.

Ambulant, walking.

Ancred (anchored), applied to a cross the four extremities of which resemble the fluke of an anchor.

Antique Crown, as it is known in Scottish heraldry, has eight points and is, in appearance, the same as the Eastern Crown.

Armed, with teeth, claws, or beak of a tincture differing from the rest of the beast.

Arrondie, made circular or round.

Attired, of a horned animal (*e.g.*, a deer), rather than Armed as for a bull.

Augmentation, an honourable addition to a coat-of-arms, granted in recognition of some special service.

Banded, encircled by a band or riband (*e.g.*, round a garb).

Barbed, of a rose with small leaves between the petals. A headed arrow or spear is also termed barbed.

Barrulet, a diminutive of the bar, a quarter of its width.

Basilisk, an heraldic monster, resembling the wyvern or cockatrice, but having at the end of its tail the head of a dragon.

Basnet (basinet), an old name for a helmet.

Baston, a narrow bend sinister, not reaching the end of the shield.

Bâton, a rod of office. (The Earl Marshal's bâton is gold tipped with black.)

Bendlet, a diminutive of the bend, one half its width.

Bendy, a field or charge divided diagonally into four, six, eight, or more equal parts, alternately tinctured.

Bezant (besant), a gold roundel: in English heraldry, like the plate, it is flat and not spherical like the other roundels. It is derived from the golden coin of Byzantium.

Bezantée, with bezants scattered over field or charge.

Billetée, with billets scattered over field or charge.

Botonnée, applied to a cross whose ends resemble the trefoil.

Bowed, embowed or arched.

Brock, a badger.

Burgonet, a kind of steel cap, worn in the sixteenth century by foot soldiers in battle.

Cabossed (caboshed), applied to the head of a beast looking out of the field, full-faced, with nothing of the neck visible.

Caltrap, an instrument of war designed to lame horses—however placed, one spike always points upward.

Cameleopard, a giraffe.

Caparison, the trappings of a horse; the saddle and harness.

Casque (healme), a helmet.

Castle, represented in heraldry by two towers with a wall between them, the wall and towers are embattled, and there is a gateway or entrance. In a three-towered castle the third tower can be seen behind the gateway.

Catherine-wheel, an instrument of torture on which St Catherine of Alexandria suffered. It therefore takes its name from the saint. A Catherine-wheel has iron teeth.

Celestial Crown, an Eastern Crown or Antique Crown, with a mullet on each point.

Chaplet, a garland of flowers and leaves.

Chequy (checky), a field divided into squares like a chess-board.

Chess-rook (*see* **Zule**).

Cinquefoil, a conventional flower with its five petals radiating from a ball.

Cognizance, a badge.

Combatant, fighting face to face.

Confrontée, facing each other.

Conjoined in Lure, applied to two wings joined together with their tips downward; used by falconers as a decoy.

Corbie, a raven.

Cornish chough, a bird of the raven family (the king of crows), often depicted with red beak and legs.

Counterflory, a tressure flory, in which alternate fleur-de-lis are reversed.

Courant, running at full speed.

Coward, an animal is termed coward in heraldry when it has its tail between its legs.

Court of Chivalry, instituted in the time of Edward III (perhaps even earlier) under constable and marshal. It dealt with military offences and questions relating to arms.

Crosier, the staff of a prelate.

Dancettée (dansée), deeply indented; when a division line is dancettée there should be no more than three indentations.

Defamed, without a tail.

Dejected, an old term for anything thrown down.

Demi, the upper (dexter) half.

Dormant, sleeping (different from couchant, as here the head rests upon the forepaws).

Double-queued, having two tails.

Eastern Crown, the crown formerly worn by Jewish kings.

Electoral Bonnet (Cap), a red cap turned up with ermine, its upper edge dancettée. It is the insignia of an Elector of the Holy Roman Empire, and it is sometimes seen in English heraldry placed over the arms of Hanover before 1814.

Embowed (embued), bent or bowed.
Endorse, a diminutive of the pale, of which it is the fourth part.
Ensigned, adorned; having a coronet, cap, cross, etc., placed above.
Epaulier, shoulder armour.
Equipped, said of horse when furnished with all its trappings.
Eradicated, violently torn up by the roots; a tree is frequently eradicated.
Erased, with a jagged edge, as opposed to couped.
Erminois, a fur-like ermine, but yellow with black spots.
Escarbuncle, a precious stone, shown in heraldry by eight sceptres emerging from a central annulet.
Fan, a common type of crest seen on early seals.
Feathered (flighted), said of arrows when the plume is of a different tincture from the shafts.
Fillet, a diminutive of the chief.
Fimbriated, edged with a different tincture. It overcomes the difficulty of placing one colour over another, or a metal upon a metal. The Union Jack is a good example of fimbriation.
Fitchée (fitchy), pointed at lower end, especially of a cross.
Fountain, a roundel barry wavy of six, argent and azure.
Fourchée, divided at the end; forked.
Fructed, bearing fruit.
Gamb (jamb, jambe), the whole foreleg of a lion or other beast.
Gauntlet, an iron glove.
Gaze (at), of a deer when standing and looking at the spectator.
Gemels, a pair of barrulets placed parallel to each other.
Genet, a small animal like a fox.
Gonfannon, a name sometimes used for a small pennon on the knight's lance.
Gorges, a whirlpool.
Gorget, armour for the throat.
Gouttée (guttée), sprinkled with drops.
Greave, armour for the leg.
Griffin-male, as the griffin, but without wings.
Guidon, a small standard.
Hauriant (haurient), of a fish when upright, as if with head above water, drawing in air.
Hawk's bells and jesses, the bells are secured to the hawk's legs by leather thongs called jesses.
Hurt, a blue roundel.

Hydra, a many-headed dragon.

In pride, applied to a peacock, or turkey cock, when its tail is displayed.

Issuant (issuing), rising from, or coming out of.

Jupon, another name for a surcoat.

Knots, differently formed, these are borne by well-known families.

Langued, said of a beast when its tongue is of a different tincture from the body.

Lioncel (lionel), small lion; usually so called when there are more than three lions.

Lozengy, covered with lozenges.

Luce, a pike (*fish*).

Main, a hand.

Manch (maunch), an old-fashioned sleeve, with long hanging ends.

Mermaid, in heraldry she generally holds a mirror in one hand and a comb in the other.

Merman, in heraldry the sea-man, or triton, is sometimes armed with sword, helmet, and breastplate.

Naiant (natant), swimming; said of a fish when borne horizontally.

Naissant, issuing from the middle of an ordinary.

Nowed, knotted; said of all creatures such as serpents and dragons, whose bodies and tails are tied into a knot.

Ogress, the same as pellet—a black roundel.

Ombré, shadowed.

Orlée, bordered.

Overt, applied to wings of birds when open for taking flight.

Pallet, a diminutive of the pale, and one-half its width.

Paly, divided by a number of vertical lines, the specified number of spaces are alternatively of a metal and a colour.

Party per pale, said of a field or charge divided equally by a vertical line, also per fesse, per saltire, per bend, and per chevron.

Pater noster, a cross composed of beads.

Pattes, the paws of any beast.

Pelican, always shown with neck bowed, pecking at her breast, and wings addorsed. Drops of blood fall from her breast, and she is blazoned as "in her piety" when feeding her young in this way.

Perforated, with the centre cut out; voided or pierced.

Pheon, the barbed head of a dart or arrow.

Phoenix, an imaginary bird; always depicted as issuing from flames.

Pierced, perforated and showing the field through aperture.

Pilgrim's scrip, a small bag worn by pilgrims, often shown with pilgrim's, or palmer's, staff.
Poing, the hand closed, as opposed to appaumée.
Pomme, a green roundel—spherical.
Popinjay, a small green parrot, with red beak and legs.
Python, a winged serpent.
Quatrefoil, a four-leaved grass with no stalk.
Queue, the tail of an animal.
Queue-fourchée, with forked tail.
Rays, sixteen in number when depicted round the sun, nine round an estoile; they must be straight and waved alternately.
Rebus, in heraldry a coat which by its charges alludes to the name of the bearer; in Westminster Abbey, Islip Chantry Chapel, carved rebus of Abbot Islip—an eye and a slip; a boy ("I") slipping from a tree.
Reflexed, turned or bent backward.
Riband (ribbon), a diminutive (one-eighth) of the bend.
Rising, of birds preparing to take flight.
Salient, a similar position to rampant, but with both hind-feet on the ground.
Savage (wild man), a man, naked, bearded, with wreaths round head and loins, and holding a club. The Duke of Edinburgh has a savage as a supporter.
Sea horse, a horse with webbed fore-feet, a fin for a mane, and its hinder parts in the form of a fish.
Sea lion, usually a beast with the upper part of a lion and the lower part of a fish.
Seeded, a term used of the seed of lilies, roses, etc., when borne of a tincture different from the flower itself.
Stock, a stump of a tree.
Sun, in heraldry is shown with a human face, and surrounded by sixteen rays, alternately straight and wavy, when it is termed "a sun in splendour," or "in full glory." Unless otherwise stated, it is of gold.
Torteau, a red roundel—spherical.
Tower, a circular embattled building with a door or port; like a chess-rook or castle.
Trefoil, a three-leaved grass with short stalk.
Trippant, applied to stag, instead of passant.
Undée (undy, ondy), wavy.
Urchin, a hedgehog.

Urinant, of a fish vertically placed with head downward; the opposite of hauriant.

Vambraced, an arm covered with armour.

Vested, clothed.

Vorant, devouring or swallowing.

Vulned, wounded and bleeding.

Wild man (*see* **Savage**).

Wood, a small group of trees growing on a mount.

Zule (Chess-rook), a piece used in the game of chess.

Index

Note: Adjectival terms—such as *addorsed*, *appaumée*, etc.—are listed alphabetically in the Glossary.